COMMUNITY COLLEGE

trustees

LEADING ON BEHALF OF THEIR COMMUNITIES

George B. Vaughan and Iris M. Weisman

ASSOCIATION OF COMMUNITY COLLEGE TRUSTEES

Community College Trustees: Leading on Behalf of Their Communities
by George B. Vaughan and Iris M. Weisman

Copyright © 1997 by the Association of Community College Trustees

Published by:
Association of Community College Trustees
1740 "N" Street, NW
Washington, DC 20036

A Special Project of the ACCT Trust Fund

Library of Congress Catalog Card Number: 97-72870

ISBN 1-886237-02-6

Printed in the United States of America

Dedicated to the trustees
of the nation's community colleges

TABLE OF CONTENTS

INTRODUCTION

This book is for community college trustees. Although the information contained in the following pages is sought by many others, the book is for trustees — and trusteeship.

First and foremost, it is intended to satisfy the continuing need trustees have to affiliate with, spend time with, share with, and learn from each other. It is intended to help trustees better understand themselves and their 6,000 or so colleagues throughout the nation. In reading these pages, trustees will discover that their many individual differences in social, economic, political and regional backgrounds all but disappear when they are functioning in their roles as board members. They will find that when acting on behalf of the community, contributing to and leading the college, trustees exhibit a strikingly similar set of values, attitudes, motivations, and goals. Trustees will also find that their colleagues share their understanding and appreciation of the role of their leadership partner, the college CEO. They will find in each other a common dedication to excellence in fulfilling the college mission and a mutual, relentless pursuit of improved governance through in-service education.

This book is also a means for trustees to communicate "who they are" to many individuals within the community college family, and to those professors of education, students, journalists, policymakers, and others whose constant curiosity about trustees is based on a desire to pursue their professional interests, well-informed about those who govern.

It may also serve as an answer to those whose questions about trustees are based on a belief that there is something wrong with community college governance, and that effective trustees may be, at least in part, the product of the selection process. It has been suggested that some sort of hierarchy exists among trustees according to three general methods of selection: Trustees appointed by elected officials are considered "too political," and trustees who attain their seats by election are said to be "ego driven or self-interested," while at the top, according to some critics, are trustees selected by the board itself, who "understand the academic community, share its values, appreciate its culture, and support the college when representing it to the public."

In addition to the misguided notion that there is a better basis for the establishment of governance than the democratic principle of popular election, some critics appear to hold the questionable view that quality trustees are focused on what is held in trust (the college), not who the trust is held for (the community). The community college exists to serve the community. Trustees should represent the values and culture of that community in their role as board members, working through the CEO who brings the culture and values of the internal college community to the table.

That community college trustees exhibit the characteristics, values, skills, and commitment to effectively govern is demonstrated by this excellent work by George Vaughan and Iris Weisman. Their contribution to trusteeship is substantial and for that effort, we are truly grateful.

Ray Taylor
ACCT President
Washington, DC

PREFACE

For the past couple of years, the first author and Ray Taylor, president of the Association of Community College Trustees (ACCT), discussed the need for a comprehensive study of community college trustees. The need to understand and appreciate the important services performed by those who govern the nation's community colleges became increasingly important as community colleges themselves became more important in meeting the educational needs of the nation. We agreed to do the study. The ACCT Trust Fund would provide some funding, and the first author would seek a second author to help with the analysis of the surveys and with the writing of the book.

Recognizing the close relationship between trustees and presidents, it was agreed that in addition to seeking the views of trustees, we would seek the views of presidents, which would add greatly to the understanding of the trustee's role. The following is what we believe to be the most comprehensive study of community college trustees conducted to date.

The study that lead to the writing of this book was conducted using two separate yet complementary research methods: mail surveys and telephone interviews. A large sample of community college presidents, board chairs, and non-chair trustees was surveyed by mail; selected presidents, board chairs, and non-chair trustees were interviewed by the first author.

Chapter 1 introduces the reader to community college boards through a presentation of the historical context of American higher education governing boards. In addition, this chapter raises a number of questions regarding community college trustees, their relationship to each other, and their relationship to their presidents. The chapter serves to establish the framework for the rest of the book.

Demographic characteristics of trustees are the focus of chapter 2. A profile of community college trustees in general is presented, followed by a comparison of board chairs to non-chair trustees, male trustees to female trustees, and Caucasian trustees to those of ethnic and racial minority groups.

In chapter 3, the very important trustee-president team is explored. Topics such as building the trustee-president team, trustees' perceptions of presidents, and presidents' perceptions of trustees are presented through first-hand experiences and perspectives of current community college trustees and presidents.

Chapter 4 presents an investigation of what trustees do "on the job" and their perceptions of these activities. In addition, certain board functions are discussed, such as trustee orientation and presidential selection.

The relationship of trustees to their communities is the topic of chapter 5. In particular, issues such as representing and communicating with the community are addressed.

In chapter 6, trustees present in their own words the satisfactions they receive from serving on a community college board.

Chapter 7 is entitled "The Perfect Fit." Trustees' perceptions of what constitutes the ideal president and presidents' perceptions of what constitutes the ideal governing board are presented.

Chapter 8 considers the influences on the trustee's role, such as board expectations, goals, and assessment. Strategies for improving the effectiveness of trustees' individual performances as well as that of community college governing boards are also presented.

The final chapter summarizes the data presented in the previous eight chapters by means of observations and recommendations. The book ends with trustees' and presidents' comments on issues facing community college boards.

One final note: the purpose of this study was to learn more about who trustees are—as individuals and as a group—and to learn about their perceptions of matters relating to community college boards. The book is not intended to be a "how-to" manual on being a community college trustee. Nevertheless, throughout the text there are lessons to be learned from the shared experiences of chairs, non-chair trustees, and presidents. In addition, the final chapter provides the authors' recommendations for community college boards and presidents.

Methodology

Three distinct survey instruments were used in this study: one for board chairs, one for non-chair trustees, and one for presidents. The trustee survey (TS) contained 64 questions, organized into seven areas: (1) trustees' activities; (2) trustees' perceptions about their boards; (3) trustees' perceptions about board members in general; (4) trustees' perceptions about board-president relations; (5) trustees' perceptions about board assessment; (6) trustees' perceptions about presidential selection; and (7) trustees' individual demographic characteristics. One final question asked trustees to state what they find most rewarding about serving as a community college trustee.

The board chair survey (CS) contained 99 questions, including the 64 asked of non-chair trustees. Five additional areas—focusing on what is done, as opposed to what is perceived—were studied through the responses of board chairs: (1) board composition and the role of the board chair; (2) board practices; (3) board assessment; (4) presidential selection processes; and (5) board evaluation of the president. Chairs were also asked to state what they find most rewarding about serving as a community college trustee.

The president survey (PS) contained 55 questions in the following categories: (1) institutional information; (2) presidents' perceptions about their boards; (3) presidents' perceptions about board members; (4) presidents' perceptions about board-president relations; and (5) presidents' perceptions about board assessment. Presidents were also asked to provide insight into their views of the relationship between their effectiveness and their board's effectiveness.

The surveys were pilot tested using presidents, governing board chairs, and other trustees. Completed surveys were analyzed for responses received to assure reliability of the questions. Participants in the pilot test were also asked to provide comments regarding the clarity and completeness of the questions and ease of completion of the survey instrument. Adjustments to the survey instruments were made based upon these comments.

The populations for this study were the presidents, board chairs, and trustees of community college governing boards whose institutions belong to the Association of Community College Trustees (ACCT). At the time of the study, a total of 517 United States governing boards, representing approximately 900 community colleges, held membership in ACCT. The following factors were considered, resulting in a reduced number of institutions included in this study: Only *governing* boards from public community colleges in the United States and its territories were studied. In states where the governing board is at the state level and the local board is *advisory*, only the state board was surveyed. Because the study focused on community colleges, branch colleges of universities were also eliminated. In addition, due to a major reorganization of the community college governing board system in one state—which occurred simultaneously with the mailing of the survey instruments—all institutions from that state were removed from the list. The final number of institutions whose presidents, board chairs, and trustees were surveyed was 505.

The president and governing board chair from the 505 selected institutions were surveyed. In addition, 20% of the non-chair trustees of each board, with a minimum of two non-chair trustees from each institution, were randomly selected and surveyed. (Student trustees and ex-officio board members were excluded from the non-chair trustee pool.)

The surveys were sent to 505 presidents, 505 board chairs, and 1063 non-chair trustees in May 1995. Follow-up postcards were mailed to non-respondents in June 1995. An overall usable response rate of 44.2% occurred, with the group breakdown as follows: 59.2% (299) of the presidents responded, 33.8% (171) of the chairs responded, and 42.1% (447) of the trustees responded.

Following the analysis of the survey data, the first author conducted in-depth telephone interviews with 15 trustees and 10 presidents selected by the ACCT staff.

Throughout the text, material based on the written surveys will be followed by their abbreviations in parentheses: CS (chair survey), PS (president survey), or TS (non-chair trustee survey). When data from the trustee survey and the chair survey were combined to obtain aggregate information about trustees in general, the abbreviation CTS is used. Except where indicated, quotes from community college trustees and presidents are taken from the telephone interviews.

Throughout the book, the term trustee is used to mean any member of the governing board, regardless of role (chair or non-chair), unless otherwise indicated in the text. The term president is also used throughout, although some individuals may have titles of chancellor, superintendent-president, or director.

Acknowledgements

The authors have been fortunate indeed to receive the support and assistance of a number of capable and generous individuals throughout the preparation of this book. We deeply and sincerely appreciate the assistance of the trustees and presidents who took the time to share their knowledge and experiences with us. Without their assistance, the book simply could not have been completed.

The first author has been very fortunate over the years in being able to work with Peggy Vaughan. In his writings he has had one rule he has never broken: Nothing is ready to be mailed until Peggy says it is ready. Peggy read and commented on the full manuscript; her knowledge of the community college is vast and her comments insightful. The second author joins in thanking Peggy for her assistance throughout the development of this manuscript.

The second author received encouragement and unwavering support from Ken Wayland. His confidence in the project was steadfast and his patience with the process was unending. Ken provided the right food at the right time—to nourish the body, mind, and soul.

The authors are fortunate to work with Barbara Scott. Barbara is managing editor of the *Community College Review*. She is a superb editor and a joy to work with. Knowing this, we asked her to read the entire manuscript. Her knowledge and outstanding skills improved the manuscript in every respect. Barbara, thank you.

Thanks are also owed to L. Louise Van Osdol of Eagle River Technologies for lending her time, skills, sense of humor, and support to this project.

Any work of this nature requires numerous revisions. The current manuscript was no exception. We will always be indebted to Carmen Sasser for the time, care, and exceptional work she did in helping us with revisions to the book.

Last, but certainly not least, we express our deep appreciation to Ray Taylor, president of the Association of Community College Trustees, for his interest in and support of the study. Ray arranged for the interviews with trustees and presidents and lent his support and endorsement to the surveys. In addition to President Taylor, we received wonderful support and encouragement from Sally Hutchins, who directs communications for ACCT, by her thorough reading of the manuscript and her editorial comments, which helped prepare the manuscript for publication.

George B. Vaughan
Iris M. Weisman
Raleigh, North Carolina

George B. Vaughan is Professor of Higher Education and Editor of the *Community College Review* at North Carolina State University. Prior to becoming a professor, he served as a community college president for 17 years. He has written a number of books and articles on the community college, including the *Community College Presidency*. He received the 1996 National Leadership Award from the American Association of Community Colleges.

Iris M. Weisman is a research and teaching associate for the Academy for Community College Leadership Advancement, Innovation, and Modeling (ACCLAIM) in the Department of Adult and Community College Education at North Carolina State University, where she completed her doctorate in community college leadership. She is the former Director of Curriculum Services for Pima Community College, Tucson, Arizona.

LIST OF FIGURES

Community College Trustees in America: Extending a Heritage

Community college trustees are important people. The 6,500 men and women who serve on the governing boards of the nation's 1,100 or so public community colleges have the legal and ethical responsibility of overseeing a seemingly endless number of academic programs, as well as approving faculty appointments, promotions, tenure, and salaries. Trustees shape long-range plans, mission statements, and college policies.

In the process, these trustees approve the expenditure of billions of dollars of public money. They also select community college presidents who serve at the pleasure of the board. Trustees do indeed hold the nation's community colleges in public trust.

Community college trustees also hold in trust the educational experiences of the more than five million students who enroll in credit courses each year at the nation's community colleges. The students depend upon trustees to obtain public support and provide guidance for the college. As trustees soon realize, public community colleges, regardless of size and location, are complex organizations that occupy a special place in the nation's higher education system. Enrolling students from almost all walks of life in credit courses, community colleges hold out the only hope many Americans have of obtaining a higher education. Committed to open access and equity in admissions, to comprehensive programs, to serving the communities in which they are located, to teaching rather than research, and to lifelong learning, these colleges have played a major role in moving the nation toward its post–World War II dream of universal higher education for all Americans. Today, because of the nation's community colleges, the dream has become a reality for many Americans—minorities, women, older adults, the disadvantaged, and the academically ill-prepared—who in the past had almost no chance of enrolling in higher education. For example, almost 50% of all first-time college students in the nation enroll in community colleges, and more than 45% of the minority students enrolled in higher education in the United States attend a community college.

Offering courses and programs in occupational-technical education, college transfer education, and developmental education, along with a vast array of community services and continuing education programs and courses, community colleges often serve as the educational hub of their communities with many also serving as cultural, social, and recreational hubs. Community college trustees, then, have the awesome and complex task of guiding and guarding what is aptly referred to as the people's college. If the community college is to remain true to its mission, trustees must assure that it remains true to its commitments to open access and comprehensiveness, thereby helping to assure that equality of educational opportunity is available for all segments of society.

Community college trustees invest their time, energy, knowledge, experience, and talents in improving their community colleges, thereby improving the quality of life of millions of individuals, of countless communities across the nation, and of the nation itself. Most community college trustees consider the community college a special institution and consider serving on its board a special privilege.

The Rise of Lay Governing Boards

Before turning specifically to community college trustees, a brief look at the development of college and university boards in general is in order. This brief look may help the reader to appreciate and more clearly understand the role of lay boards in American higher education and, in turn, to view the role of community college boards through the broader perspective of higher education as a whole.

America's system of higher education is the envy of the world, for no other nation has achieved the combination of equity and excellence found in our institutions. One of the major strengths and distinguishing characteristics of American higher education is its control by lay governing boards. Lay boards of higher education remain at the heart of American higher education and, for the most part, are highly effective. As Clark Kerr notes, "The basic governance system of American higher education is, I believe, the best in the world—with great responsibility placed with independent boards of trustees" (Kerr, 1994, p. 36). The system of lay control, so firmly entrenched today, was arrived at slowly and, in some cases, only after much struggle.

Prior to the American Revolution, the fight for control of the Colonial colleges was often one between faculty control and external control. In the early Colonial colleges, the clergy exercised both internal control as presidents and external control as trustees. Gradually, however, the clergy lost their positions as college presidents to secular leaders in most institutions, and became less important as members of governing boards, especially in nondenominational and public institutions. Clergy were replaced by "conservative men of wealth who . . . were pillars of the better classes, . . . [whose] authority also enabled them to keep the colleges true to the interests and prejudices of the classes from which they were drawn" (Rudolph, 1990, p. 173). By the end of the American Revolution, it seemed that control of the new nation's colleges and universities was to lie in external hands.

Francis Wayland, well-known and highly respected president of Brown University (1827–1855), supported a degree of faculty control. Although not a great supporter of external control, he was pragmatic about the public's influence. He reasoned, much as trustees and presidents reason today, that if the college obtained its financial support from the public, then the college's trustees should be responsible to the public for the actions taken on behalf of the college (Brubacher & Rudy, 1968, p. 31).

Once the argument of internal versus external control abated, the early colleges and their lay governing boards had to decide how to incorporate their institutions under public statutes while preserving the academic freedom of faculty, serving the public good, and rejecting undue influence from special interest groups, including politicians and business leaders. Early arguments about control centered around whether the college was incorporated as a private or public corporation (Brubacher & Rudy, 1968). The famous Dartmouth College case (1819) upheld that institution's right to function as a private rather than a public corporation and did much to set the stage for today's distinction between private versus public institutions.

4

Beginning with the opening of the University of Georgia in 1785 and the University of North Carolina ten years later, all of the states soon joined the movement toward establishing state universities. For example, Thomas Jefferson's University of Virginia, which opened for classes in 1825, was clearly a public institution. The lay trustees of these public institutions were legally responsible for their institutions and therefore responsible to the public for their own actions and the actions of their institutions. Moreover, lay control meant that "the President shall be elected by the Board of Regents [trustees], be responsible to it, and serve at the pleasure of the Board" (Kauffman, 1980, p. 1). Lay control of higher education institutions was clearly on the rise and remains in practice today.

Clark Kerr and Marian Gade, the authors of an important 1989 study of college and university trustees, titled their work *The Guardians: Boards of Trustees of American Colleges and Universities*. And what do these guardians protect? Kerr and Gade provide some clues: "The lay board is the primary instrument that protects autonomy, encourages competition, and balances the needs of internal and external constituencies" (p. 9). Boards that protect institutional autonomy and balance the needs of internal and external constituencies have their hands full in today's society; many individuals and forces, both external and internal to the institution, would move colleges and universities in directions that would serve special interests, interests not always in concert with the public's interests. It is the responsibility of the lay governing boards to see that the nation's colleges and universities act to promote the public good, not special interests. Trustees are truly guardians of the public trust, and the future of American higher education is in their hands.

Why Serve?

Approximately 46,000 men and women serve on the governing boards of the nation's higher education institutions (Kerr & Gade, 1989, p. 35), some serving for two decades or more. Why would anyone want to give up his or her time to serve as a trustee of an American higher education institution? What is it about America's system of higher education that draws highly talented lay men and women into serving on governing boards? Even when free from the pressure of high profile, high energy, expensive, and time-consuming activities such as seeking and selecting a new president, raising funds for a new building, setting the institution's mission and goals, or deciding what positions and curricula to add or eliminate, serving as a college or university trustee is a daunting task.

For whatever reason, serving on a college or university board of trustees is seen as a high calling in American society and as an important avenue for fulfilling one's civic responsibilities. Indeed, service on a college or university board of trustees is an important statement on American democracy; these lay boards make it possible for our institutions of higher education to function effectively in a society committed to democratic ideals. Once on the governing board, most trustees perform their duties willingly and usually without pay.

In addition to being responsible to the general public, trustees also must make decisions that affect students, faculty, and alumni. Each of these groups has its own vision of where the college should be going and how it should get there. Issues brought before some boards of trustees run the gamut from rules of student conduct, parking, food service, sports, salaries and benefits, curriculum, academic freedom, tuition costs and other sources of funding, to tenure and promotion and the perpetual need to communicate more effectively.

Serving on a community college governing board must be a labor of love, for trustees are under constant public review and are the occasional target of public criticism. Trustees may sometimes find their ethics challenged. For example, they may be asked, as a *very special favor,* to have a politician's or community leader's relative or friend appointed to the college faculty or staff. Today's governing boards of public institutions, including community colleges, are clearly accountable to the public in general and not to any special interests.

A Very Special Relationship

Most individuals who have studied how colleges are governed agree that boards and presidents who work together as a team enhance the effectiveness of their institution in achieving its goals (Kauffman, 1980; Carver & Mayhew, 1994; Walker, 1986). Trustees share with the president the responsibility of seeing that the team functions effectively and efficiently to achieve the college's mission, thus any comprehensive discussion of trustees must include a discussion of the president's role.

Effective trustees understand that they must establish, maintain, and enhance their relations with the college's president, at times serving as cheerleader, at times as friendly critic. When relations sour, as they do on occasion, trustees must dismiss the president, thereby setting into motion the expensive, time-consuming, and at times frustrating task of finding a replacement.

Nevertheless, the trustee-president relationship is the one constant in the lives of trustees. Although the players may change and the roles of trustees and presidents may change, the importance of the trustee-president relationship is as important today as it was in the past. Community college trustees have seen great changes in their roles over the past two decades as the colleges they govern have matured and as their roles as trustees have become more clearly defined. Presidents have also seen their roles change, with an increasing emphasis on working with business and industry and raising funds from private sources. What has not changed is the need for presidents and trustees to work as a team. To put it plainly: trustees and presidents need each other.

Operating in simpler times, Robert Hutchins, president of the University of Chicago (1929–1950), recognized the importance of the trustee-president relationship. When asked what advice he would give to presidents, he is said to have replied: "Take a trustee to lunch" (quoted in Walker, 1986, p. 131). One study of college and university trustees states unequivocally that the performance of a president depends on the performance of the board. "The relationship, without too much exaggeration, may be looked upon as that of Siamese twins: 'president-board' or 'board-president'" (Kerr & Gade, 1989, p. 3).

Although most trustees recognize the importance of their relationship with presidents, mistakes resulting in a less than desirable situation sometimes occur in the presidential selection process. The reaction is often similar to that of a recently married couple who, thinking they know each other well, wake up one morning and exclaim, "What happened?" Mismatches are the exception, however; most relations between the board and president are positive, and most presidents are chosen after careful screening. Indeed, almost 73% of the trustees responding to the trustees' survey feel that the degree of trust between trustees and presidents is strong (CTS).

Trustees or presidents who do not understand the importance of the relationship between the successful college and the successful trustee-president team, or who have not fulfilled the relationship in a positive way, will fail to lead their institutions effectively. These institutions cannot achieve their potential without a board and president who share and support a common vision for the institution, a vision that must be jointly shaped, articulated, and pursued.

Community College Trustees

One of the clichés that regularly makes the rounds in community college circles is that the public does not completely understand the role and mission of community colleges. The trouble with clichés is that they contain enough truth to warrant the attention of those seriously interested in the subject. There is some truth in "they don't understand us," with the "they" being anyone from high school counselors to politicians and the "us" being community colleges and their leaders. Trustees, if they are to be effective, must understand the historical role and mission of the institution they govern. The following precepts that shape the mission of most community colleges should be understood by every community college trustee:

■ a commitment to serving all segments of society through an open-access admissions policy;

9

- a commitment to a comprehensive educational program that offers programs and courses leading to employment or transfer to a four-year institution;

- a commitment, as a community-based institution, to serving the community through concern for its health and welfare;

- a commitment to teaching rather than to research; and

- a commitment to lifelong learning for all who can profit from such learning.

In addition, trustees should understand that the college's mission is more than philosophical, that programs, activities, and services are necessary to accomplish the mission. The mission in most community colleges is implemented through the following:

- college transfer programs;

- occupational-technical programs;

- developmental and remedial educational offerings;

- community services, including credit and non-credit offerings; and,

- any number of support services such as counseling, financial services, and learning resources support (Vaughan, 1995).

Commitment to the community college mission is an important reason for serving as a community college trustee. There are, however, more specific and personal reasons for serving.

Specifically, then, why would a community leader want to become a trustee of a community college, knowing full well that the position is likely to bring frustrations as well as rewards? The answers vary from individual to individual and from institution to institution. Some reasons reflect one's feelings on citizenship: "I love my country, my state, my community, and it is my responsibility to make life as good as possible for all members of society, and I can do this by helping my community college." Other reasons relate to a specific institution: "If it were not for our community college, I would not be where I am today; it gave me a chance." Other reasons are personal and may, on the surface, imply that the major reason some trustees serve is for self-aggrandizement: "I need the prestige, or contacts, or public recognition that come with service on the community college's governing board."

Serving as a member of a community college's governing board, in addition to having its own unique package of rewards and frustrations, is often hard work and consumes much time and energy. Most boards meet monthly and some as often as twice a month. Because community colleges occupy the segment of higher education that, more than any other, intersects and interacts with its community on a daily basis, the simple act of leaving one's home places the trustee face-to-face with the college's constituents and owners—the public. A result is that the community college's position in the community constantly places trustees on the firing line, making them available to all constituents essentially all of the time. Even though one hallmark of a community college is its responsiveness to its community, the constant exposure to community concerns and the expectations that come with those concerns often increases the difficulty of the trustees' role.

Commenting upon the role of community college governing boards, one long-time trustee and scholar makes the following observation:

It would be rare indeed to find a more important or more difficult role, carried out by more dedicated, selfless public servants, than that of a governing board member of a community college. With all of the passion and ability we possess, each of us undertakes the responsibility to represent our fellow citizens, and in full view of the often critical, self-interested public, exercise control over a highly complex organization in an uncertain economic and social environment, fulfill a mission that speaks to improving the quality of life, and lest we forget, demonstrate that we have been successful (George E. Potter, in Carver & Mayhew, 1994, p. v).

Although all community college governing boards are different, most community college trustees can identify with and appreciate the above observations.

It is in the milieu of lay control, public ownership, public trust, and public service that community college trustees perform their duties. Building upon proud traditions extending back to Colonial times, today's community college trustees, through their daily activities and devotion, fulfill their commitment to the community college mission. By doing so, they fulfill commitments to their communities, their states, and their nation.

Community college trustees give hours of their time to the myriad of tasks that accompany membership on the governing board. They know, or soon discover after joining the board, that community colleges, regardless of size, location, sources of funding, students served, or courses offered, are complex entities that require much care and feeding if they are to be successful.

They also discover that many individuals and groups are interested in decisions that affect their community college, regardless of how mundane some decisions may appear to be. Community members want to know and have the right to know what decisions are made, who makes them, why they are made, and what happens after they are made. Most community college trustees know this is how it should and must be, for they realize that they are the people's representatives on the board and, as such, hold the college in trust. Community college trustees, then, are important members of our society and of our higher education system. Their story of extending the heritage of lay trusteeship follows, with much of it told in their own words.

A **Profile** of

Community

College

Trustees

Community colleges are not all alike. Influenced by the political, economic, social, and technological environments in which they function, successful community colleges must be responsive to the unique needs of their communities. Funding sources and governing structures also vary among public community colleges.

Some community colleges have their governing board at the state level, some at the local level, and a few at the tribal level. The different models of governance in turn produce different structures for community college boards.

Just as every community college board is different, so are the individuals who serve on these boards. On the other hand, just as every board has some things in common, the trustees who comprise these boards have characteristics in common. Who, then, are the individuals who serve as the guardians of the nation's community colleges? The following discussion answers this question, at least in part.[1]

---

1. Note to the reader: Certain stylistic decisions were made by the authors to present clearly the information obtained from this research. As stated in the methodology section, two methods were used for this study: mail surveys and telephone interviews. Three distinct survey instruments were developed and administered: one for the board chair (CS), one for the non-chair trustee (TS), and one for the president (PS). Throughout the text, material based on the written surveys will be followed by their abbreviations in parentheses: CS, PS, or TS. When data from the trustee survey and the chair survey are combined to obtain aggregate

Characteristics

A total of 618 trustees (171 chairs and 447 non-chair trustees) from more than 380 community college boards (over 56% of all community college governing boards) responded to questions regarding their demographic characteristics (CTS). The following data provide a look at the men and women who serve as trustees of the nation's community colleges.

Gender. According to survey results, a trustee is twice as likely to be male than to be female. The responses indicate that 67% of the trustees are men and 33% are women (CTS). When compared to the results of earlier studies, these figures show a trend of increasing participation by women on community college boards (Drake, 1977; Rauh, 1969; Whitmore, 1987).

Race or Ethnicity. The predominance of Caucasians on community college boards is depicted in Figure 2.1. In descending order, the racial or ethnic composition of community college boards includes Caucasians (86.6%), African Americans (7.9%), Hispanics (2.3%), "other" (1.2%), Asian Americans (1.1%), and Native Americans (0.8%) (CTS).

Neither the gender nor race or ethnicity of trustees reflects the makeup of many of the communities served by community colleges. Is it important that community college governing boards reflect the makeup of the community which the college serves? The question is complex and will be examined in some detail later in this chapter.

information about trustees in general, the abbreviation CTS is used. Except where indicated, quotes from community college trustees and presidents are taken from the telephone interviews.

16

Figure 2.1 All trustees by race/ethnicity

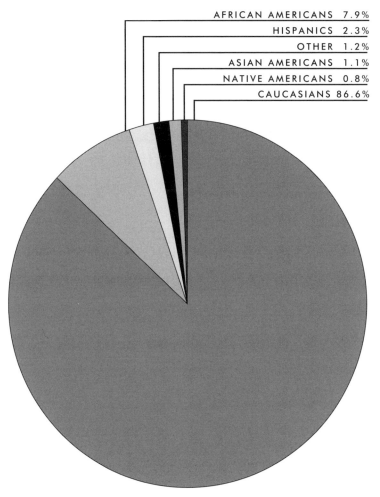

AFRICAN AMERICANS 7.9%
HISPANICS 2.3%
OTHER 1.2%
ASIAN AMERICANS 1.1%
NATIVE AMERICANS 0.8%
CAUCASIANS 86.6%

Age. A wide range of ages is represented by community college trustees, yet the scale tips toward older trustees. Of the 580 trustees who reported their age, the youngest turned 22 years old at his most recent birthday (student trustees were not included in this study) and the two oldest trustees were 84 at their most recent birthday. The most common age for trustees is 52, and the average age of trustees is 57½ years old. Approximately 5% of the trustees are under 40 years of age; 20% are in their 40s; 30% are in their 50s; 30% in their 60s; and nearly 15% are 70 or older (CTS) (see Figure 2.2).

Political Choices. The two major political parties in this country claim affiliation from 85% of the trustees, with slightly more trustees aligning themselves with the Republican Party. Forty-three percent of the trustees state that they are affiliated with the Republican Party; 42% position themselves with the Democratic Party, and 14% state that they are independents. Regardless of political party, more than half of the trustees (52%) consider themselves to be moderates; 35% of the trustees identify themselves as conservatives; and 12% declare that they are liberals (CTS).

Education. Board members have been and continue to be well-educated individuals. In 1968, 70% of the trustees had a bachelor's degree or higher (Rauh, 1969, p. 171). This proportion is increasing, with the current survey results revealing that 85% of the trustees currently have earned a bachelor's degree or higher. In fact, slightly more than one-half (51%) of the community college trustees have earned a graduate degree (CTS). (See Figure 2.9 for a comparison of educational attainment of trustees.)

What about trustees' experiences as students at the community college? Slightly more than one-half (50.8%) of the trustees stated that they had attended a community college at some time in their lives, and approximately one-third of them had earned an associate's degree (CTS). Having experience as a community college student and seeing firsthand what occurs

18

Figure 2.2 Age range of all trustees

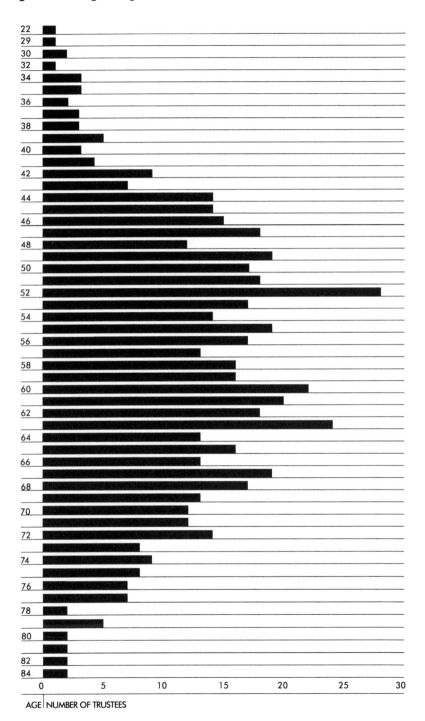

AGE | NUMBER OF TRUSTEES

in the classroom may provide trustees with a student-oriented perspective on community college governance.

Employment Status. More than 68% of community college trustees are employed outside the home on either a full-time (63%) or part-time (6%) basis. Approximately 28% of the community college trustees state that they are retired. (The age range of retired trustees covers ages 51 to 84 [CTS].)

Three percent of trustees are full-time homemakers (CTS). Of interest is that the percentage of full-time homemakers who are trustees has not changed dramatically in nearly 20 years; in 1977, 7% of community college trustees were full-time homemakers (Drake, 1977, p. 10).

Occupations. Trustees were asked to list their current occupation or, if retired, to list their last full-time occupation. In what kinds of occupations do community college trustees engage? As indicated in Figure 2.3, the categories of primary occupations are dominated by the professions (67.4%), followed by business owner or manager (16.6%). Over 4% of the trustees who responded state that they are employed in sales, service, or office work; and another 4% state that they are farmers, farm managers, or foresters. Less than 1% (0.2%) view themselves as unskilled workers (CTS).

The 406 trustees who selected the classification of professionals as their primary occupation were asked to specify in which profession they work. The categories included bankers or other financial managers, educators at all levels, engineers, scientists, attorneys, members of the clergy, social workers, psychologists, dentists, physicians, and other health professionals. Education heads the list with 37% of the 406 trustees who classified themselves

20

Figure 2.3 Primary occupations of all trustees

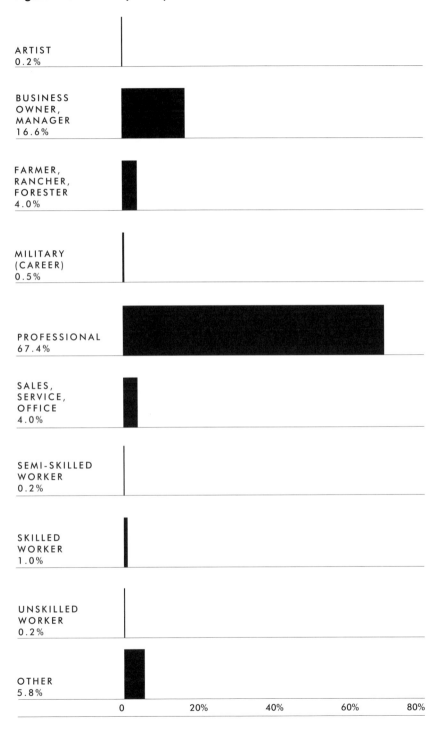

as professionals. (Twenty-four percent of the respondents work in the K–12 system, 11% in higher education, and 2% did not specify at which level they work). Twelve percent of the 406 trustees who are professionals are lawyers or judges; 11% are in the medical and other health care professions; and slightly more than 10% are in banking or finance (CTS). (See Figure 2.4.)

Interestingly, 4% of the community college trustees have taught at the community college on a full-time basis and 18% have taught part-time (CTS). Of course, teaching at the community college part-time does not necessarily mean that trustees would report their professional category as education. Lawyers, doctors, dentists, bankers, business leaders, artists, technicians, mechanics, and many others teach part-time at community colleges.

Trustees, then, represent a cross section of the community, with the majority falling under the broad category of professional. If there is a surprise, it might be in the relatively high percentage of professionals who identify themselves as educators.

Family Income. Community college trustees, regardless of occupation, appear to come from the middle and upper classes of American society. A total of 593 trustees answered a question regarding their family income. According to the survey results, nearly 77% of the trustees have an annual family income of more than $55,000. In fact, 36% of the trustees list an annual family income of at least $100,000 (CTS). Although the survey's upper limit was $100,000 or more, it is likely that many trustees' annual family incomes go well beyond the $100,000 mark.

Figure 2.4 Categories of professions of trustees who classify their occupation as professional

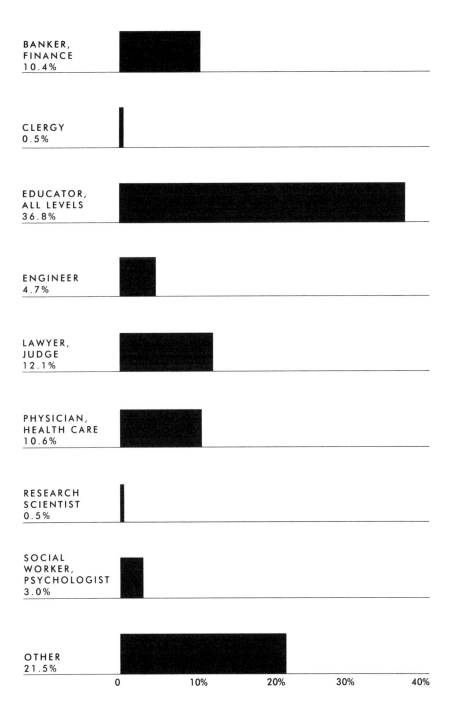

BANKER,
FINANCE
10.4%

CLERGY
0.5%

EDUCATOR,
ALL LEVELS
36.8%

ENGINEER
4.7%

LAWYER,
JUDGE
12.1%

PHYSICIAN,
HEALTH CARE
10.6%

RESEARCH
SCIENTIST
0.5%

SOCIAL
WORKER,
PSYCHOLOGIST
3.0%

OTHER
21.5%

0   10%   20%   30%   40%

A "Typical" Trustee

The above data provides enough facts and figures to give some indication of who the nation's trustees are, at least as viewed through selected categories. While generalizations beg for exceptions and while the word *typical* can never fully apply when discussing a group as diverse as the trustees of the nation's community colleges, one can make some observations about community college trustees based on the above.

The great majority of trustees are Caucasian males. Many of the trustees identify themselves as professionals. The majority of the trustees work full-time outside the home, have a relatively high family income, and are well-educated. A large percentage attended a community college, and approximately one-third of those attending received the associate's degree. The average age of trustees is 57½, with a few trustees serving into their 80s. The great majority of trustees are moderate or conservative in their political views. The above profile is useful in understanding where trustees are "coming from" and may give some clues as to where they may see the colleges they govern going in the future.

Becoming a Community College Trustee

The most common avenue through which trustees become involved with their community college board is through the political process (38%). Twenty-six percent of the trustees had been members of other boards and wanted experience on a community college board. Nearly one-quarter of the trustees (24.8%) had been encouraged by a colleague who was a trustee, and another 12% had been encouraged by a college president to serve on the governing board. As noted earlier, slightly over 50% of community college trustees have attended a community college. This was also an impetus for becoming a trustee. More than 13% of the trustees stated that they had been community college students and wanted to give something back to their institutions (CTS). Figure 2.5 depicts the various ways through which trustees become involved with the community college board. (Note: Trustees were asked to identify all the reasons for becoming involved with the community college board; therefore, the total exceeds 100%.)

Figure 2.5   Why and how trustees become involved with the community college

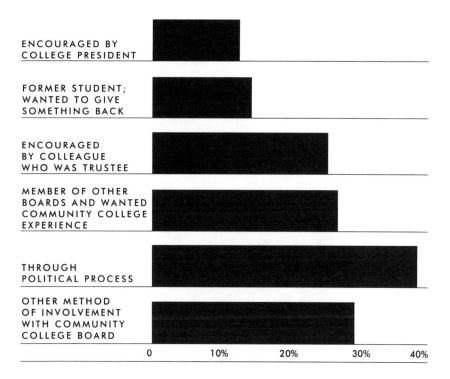

25

After someone acknowledges his or her desire to become a community college trustee, how does one go about the business of being selected to serve on the board? Board chairs were asked to describe all the ways in which trustees are selected for their board. In descending order, the most frequent methods are appointment by the governor (35.1%), district-wide elections (30.4%), and appointment by local elected officials (28.1%) (CTS). Figure 2.6 displays the various ways in which trustees are selected. (Because many boards have more than one method for selecting trustees, the total exceeds 100%.)

Figure 2.6   Percent of boards using various methods of trustee selection

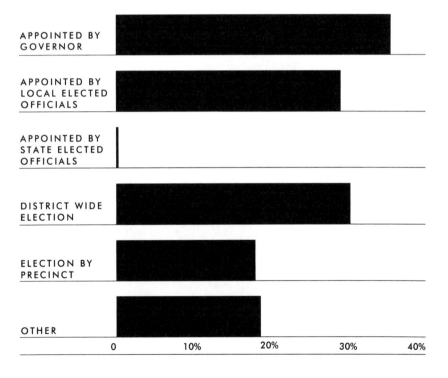

Others on the Board. Does anyone other than community college trustees sit on the board? Board chairs responded to questions regarding the status of students and faculty on their boards. The data show that on 44.7% of the boards, students serve alongside trustees. Of those boards who have student trustees, 39.2% award voting privileges to the students. Only 2.4% of the boards have faculty members who sit on the board; none of these faculty members have voting privileges (CS).

Length of Service. How long does a typical trustee serve on a community college board? At the time of the survey, the average length of time that the trustees had served on their boards was 8.7 years (CTS). Board chairs spent more years on the board than non-chairs, with the average tenure of chairs at 10.6 years, and the average tenure of non-chairs at 8.0 years (CS; TS).

Becoming a Chair. How does a trustee become a chair? In the 171 institutions whose chairs responded to our survey, by far the most common method for selecting a chair is by trustee vote. Ninety-seven percent of the chairs state that board chairs are elected by the board members. Chair terms are short in duration; over 93% of the chairs' terms are two years or less, although most institutions (92%) allow chairs to serve consecutive terms (CS). Thus, the actual time someone serves as chair may extend well beyond the two-year term. Since the board chair plays an important role on most boards, a closer look needs to be taken at the chair.

Board Chairs: Are They Different?

The designated leader of the board is its chair. The chair participates in shaping the agenda and presides over board meetings. John W. Nason, a leading authority on college trustees, has the following to say about the role of the board chair: "In both the public and the private sectors [of higher education] the chairman must moderate as well as lead—a healer of breaches, harmonizer of divisiveness, sometimes cajoler and, when necessary, a disciplinarian. To the public the chairman is the symbol of the board and very often its spokesman. Within the board the chairman sets the example for the other trustees by his or her personal performance" (Nason, 1982, p. 83).

How different are board chairs from non-chair trustees? Based upon the responses to the survey, there are many similarities between chairs and non-chairs. By the same token, differences between chairs and non-chairs surfaced from the survey data and deserve to be mentioned. The next section presents a comparison of these two categories of board members. (It is important to remember that the data presented earlier in this chapter represent the combined responses of the 618 trustees who completed the survey. In the next section, two separate data sets are compared: responses from 171 chairs versus responses from 447 non-chairs.)

Gender and Race or Ethnicity. Chairs and non-chairs are more similar to each other in terms of race or ethnicity than they are in terms of gender. Of the 166 chairs who responded to the question about gender, 42 (25.3%) are women; whereas of the 440 non-chair trustees who responded to the same question, 156 (35.5%) are women. For both chairs and non-chairs, the great majority of trustees are Caucasian—89.1% of the chairs and 85.6% of the non-chairs. African Americans top the list of the racial or ethnic minorities, constituting 7% of the chairs and 8% of the non-chairs (CS; TS).

Political Choices. There are some political differences between chairs and non-chairs. Whereas non-chairs tend to have greater party affiliation with the Democrats (44%), chairs tend to align with the Republicans (54%). Approximately one half of both groups (50.6% of the chairs and 52.6% of the non-chairs) state that they are moderate in ideology (CS; TS).

Employment Status and Occupation. The survey data reveal a similar employment pattern between chairs and non-chairs. Over 60% of both groups are employed full-time outside the home. Chairs (25%) are slightly less likely than non-chairs (29%) to be retired. In addition, the proportion of trustees who are homemakers does not greatly differ between chairs and nonchairs (CS; TS).

Chairs and non-chair trustees tend to be employed in the same occupational fields. The most common occupation for chairs and non-chairs is in the professions. Business owner and manager is the second most frequently identified occupation for both chairs and non-chairs (CS; TS).

Age. Chairs are slightly older than non-chairs. The average age of a chair (59) is nearly two years older than the average age for non-chairs (57) (CS; TS).

Family Income. There are some differences in annual family income between chairs and non-chairs. Fewer chairs have family incomes of $70,000 or less (30% of the chairs versus 37% of the non-chairs); yet 36% of both chairs and non-chairs reveal family incomes of more than $100,000 per year (CS; TS).

Community college trustees as a whole do not constitute a homogeneous group. As explored above, one way of differentiating among trustees is by their role as chair or non-chair on the board. The study results reveal that there are relatively few differences between chairs and non-chairs regarding their demographic characteristics. Are there other ways in which trustees may be alike or different? In keeping with the current research on diversity in community colleges, the two categories of gender and race or ethnicity were identified as important areas to study. The responses to the survey were analyzed in order to compare the characteristics of men to the characteristics of women, and the characteristics of Caucasians to the characteristics of people from racial or ethnic minorities. (For the rest of this chapter, the combined data of all 618 trustees—chairs and non-chairs—are presented.)

Comparing Men and Women

Of the 606 trustees who responded to the question on gender, 198 were women and 408 were men (CTS). (Twelve respondents declined to specify their gender, and, therefore, their responses could not be included in this portion of the data analysis.) As one can see, the ratio of women to men is approximately 1 to 2. A comparison of some of their demographic characteristics follows.

Race or Ethnicity. A higher percentage of men are Caucasian (88%) than are women (84%). African Americans constitute the largest minority subgroup for both men and women, making up nearly 6% of the male trustees and over 11% of the female trustees. In terms of representation, a gap exists between African Americans and other minority groups. Hispanics constitute 3% of the female trustees and 2% of the male trustees. There are no Asian American women among the survey respondents; less than 2% of the male trustees are Asian American. Native Americans constitute 1% of the female trustees and less than 1% of the male trustees (CTS). (See Figure 2.7 for a comparison of the racial or ethnic breakdown of the female and male trustees.)

Figure 2.7 Racial/ethnic breakdown of female and male trustees

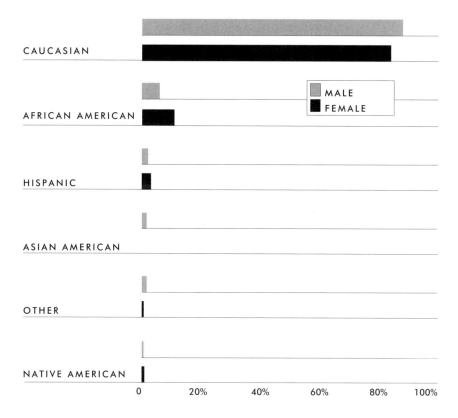

Political Preferences. As shown in Figure 2.8, there is a decided political difference between men and women. Whereas more women tend to be Democrats (53.6% of the female trustees are Democrats; 32% are Republicans; and 12.4% are Independents), more men tend to be Republicans (48.1% of the male trustees are Republicans; 35.7% are Democrats; and 15.2% are Independents). Regardless of political party affiliation, men tend to be ideologically more conservative than women (41.6% of the male trustees

Figure 2.8   Political preferences of female and male trustees

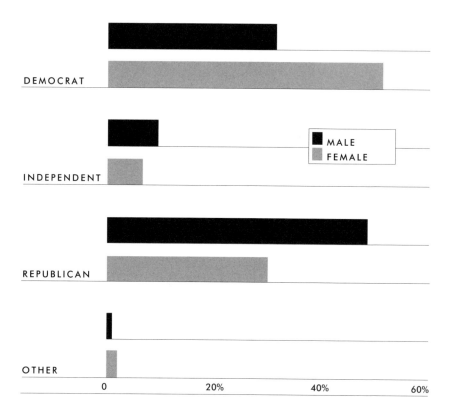

versus 20.2% of the female trustees state that they are conservative). Over 60% of the women consider themselves moderate, and 48% of the men consider themselves moderate. Women are twice as likely as men to call themselves liberal (18% of the female trustees versus 9% of the male trustees) (CTS).

Employment Characteristics. A greater percentage of men (73.8%) than women (58.2%) work outside the home. Conversely, only female trustees list their occupation as homemakers; almost 8.7% of female trustees are in this category. In addition, 31.1% of all female trustees are retired, whereas 26% of all male trustees are retired (CTS).

Men and women have similar occupations. The majority of both men and women show a preponderance of employment as professionals (69% for women and 67% for men). The second most prevalent occupation for both groups is business owner or manager (CTS).

The category of professions with the largest percentage of trustees is the same for both men and women: education. Nearly one half (49.7%) of the female trustees and slightly more than 30% of the male trustees who classify their occupation as professional, are educators, primarily in the K–12 system. Slightly over one third (36.1%) of the female trustees who are educators and 17.8% of the male trustees who are educators state that they work in the K–12 system (CTS).

Education. Over 60% of the female trustees and nearly 47% of the male trustees have attended a community college. Approximately 34% of the men and 30% of the women who attended a community college earned an associate's degree (CTS).

The educational levels of male and female trustees were also compared. (See Figure 2.9 for a breakdown of educational attainment by gender and race or ethnicity.) More men (87.5%) than women (81.2%) earned a bachelor's degree or higher. Yet, 32% of the women and 26% of the men completed the master's degree as their highest degree. Moreover, 9% of the women and 8% of the men attained their doctorates (Ph.D. or Ed.D.), yet men outnumbered women (18% compared to 3%) in earning professional degrees such as J.D., M.D., D.V.M., and D.D.S. (CTS).

Age. The age range for men is 22 to 84, while the age range for women is 35 to 79. The average age for both men and women is approximately 57 years old, yet the most common age for men is 52 and the most common age for women is 55 (CTS).

Family Income. Male trustees appear to come from families who are slightly better off economically than the families of female trustees. Eight percent of men have an annual family income of $40,000 or less, whereas nearly 16% of women come from that same income bracket. More than one-third of both male and female trustees have family incomes of more than $100,000 per year.

In reviewing the above statistics, it becomes apparent that, in general, trustees differ somewhat by gender. The main areas of distinction seem to be that more women are from minority groups, men tend to be more politically conservative than women, and men tend to be employed outside the home more frequently than are women.

Comparing Caucasians and Minority Groups[2]

Gender is not the only method of differentiating between community college trustees. What can be learned about trustees by looking at them accord-

---

2. Another stylistic decision that the authors made concerned the use of the term *minorities*. For the purposes of this book, minorities include the following racial or ethnic groups: African Americans, Asian Americans, Hispanics, Native Americans, and "other" groups, following the categories by which the trustees identified themselves on the survey.

ing to their race or ethnicity? As mentioned earlier, of the 604 trustees who responded to the question regarding their race or ethnicity, 523 trustees (86.6%) are Caucasian. The remaining 81 respondents fall into the following categories: 48 African American trustees (7.9%), 14 Hispanic trustees (2.3%), 7 Asian American trustees (1.2%), 5 Native American trustees (0.8%), and 7 "other" trustees (1.2%) (CTS).

Gender. The gender breakdown between Caucasian trustees and trustees from minority groups is similar to the total percentages of male (67%) and female (33%) trustees. Women constitute 39% of the minority trustees and 32% of the Caucasian trustees (CTS).

Political Preferences. According to the survey responses, Caucasian trustees are more conservative politically than are minority trustees. Almost 14% of minority trustees consider themselves to be conservative, while 37% of the Caucasians claim this political ideology. Approximately 65% of the minority trustees are Democrats, and approximately 19% are Republicans. This compares to the nearly 38% of the Caucasian trustees who are Democrats and approximately 47% who are Republicans (CTS).

Employment Status. The employment profiles of Caucasians and minorities vary. In both groups, over 60% of the trustees work full-time; 33% percent of the minority trustees and approximately 27% of the Caucasian trustees are retired (CTS). Minority trustees, however, have a higher percentage of people employed in the professions. Nearly 66% of the Caucasians state that they are employed as professionals, while 79% of the minorities selected the professions as their primary occupation. Fifty percent of the minority trustees and 34% of the Caucasian trustees who classify their occupation as professional, were employed in education. After the professions, the most common primary occupation for both Caucasians and minorities is as a business owner or manager (CTS).

Education. How does the educational attainment of these groups compare? Minority trustees have achieved a higher level of formal education than have their Caucasian counterparts. Over 47% of minority trustees attended a community college, and almost 40% of those who attended graduated with an associate's degree. For the Caucasian trustees, almost 52% attended the community college, and 31% received an associate's degree. Ninety percent of the minority trustees earned a bachelor's degree or higher, as compared to 85% of Caucasian trustees. Moreover, 69% of the minority trustees earned a master's degree or higher, whereas 48% of the Caucasians reached this level of educational attainment (CTS). (See Figure 2.9 below.)

Age. Age characteristics for people from minority groups are similar to the characteristics stated above for women. The age range for minority trustees is 32–77, and their average age is approximately 55 years old. For the Caucasians, their age range is 22–84, and their average age is approximately 58 years old (CTS).

Family Income. Caucasian trustees are financially better off than minority trustees. Whereas approximately 10% of the Caucasian trustees have annual family incomes of $40,000 or less, approximately 18% of the minority trustees fall within this income bracket. On the other end, whereas 26% of minority trustees have family incomes of $100,000 or more, 38% of the Caucasian trustees report this income level (CTS).

Figure 2.9 Highest educational level of all trustees by gender and race/ethnicity

In summary, minority trustees are less conservative, have achieved a higher level of formal education, are younger, and have lower annual family incomes than Caucasian trustees. In addition, a greater percentage of minority trustees are professional educators than are Caucasian trustees.

What conclusions can be drawn from the findings that female trustees have different characteristics than male trustees and that minority trustees have different characteristics than Caucasian trustees? The answers may lie in the issue of diversity in community college leadership.

Representing the Community

Like the community colleges they govern, trustees contribute to the processes and products of their communities, and, in turn, are shaped by them. Trustees must confront the dreams, challenges, frustrations, successes, and failures inherent in their communities, especially as these relate to community colleges. How important is it that the gender, racial or ethnic makeup of a board matches that of the community college's service area?

The debate about diversity and community representation on higher education governing boards is a long-standing one. At one end, scholars such as Zoglin (1976) and Keeton (1977) believe that the important question is whether the trustee understands and protects community concerns, not what the trustee's heritage is. "Those who protect the public interest in governing need not be altogether typical of the public they protect. The constituencies should have effective advocacy before, and response from, the board; they need not be, and cannot always be, equally well-represented on the board" (Keeton, 1977, p. 206). Those who support Keeton's statement would argue for trustees who can see beyond their own issues and work toward the common good of all members of the community.

On the other side of the debate are those scholars who do not trust the ability of a homogeneous group to know, consider, and protect the needs of people who are not "like them." For at least the last 54 years, there has been growing concern about how members of lay boards of trustees in higher education can represent constituents who differ in race, ethnicity, or gender. As far back as 1943, there was documented concern that "too many old men" (Hughes, 1943, p. 6) were on boards and that board "members should broadly represent the classes of people the institution is designed to serve" (p. 7).

Almost fifty years later, this issue was brought to the forefront by Gillett-Karam, Roueche, and Roueche (1991) in their book *Underrepresentation and the Question of Diversity*. The major issue raised by that book was how an institution whose mission is based on a philosophy of open enrollment, inclusiveness, and democracy can "make good on its promise to educate all of the people" (p. 4). Gillett-Karam, Roueche, and Roueche contend that community colleges must value diversity, pluralism, and multiculturalism, and that women and members of minority groups should be in positions of leadership in proportion to their representation in the population.

Does the community college mission's emphasis on community mean that community college trustees should reflect demographically the various groups who live in their communities? Are women and people from racial or ethnic minorities the only groups that need to be considered for the purposes of representation? Which constituencies should the community college board represent—students, employers, four-year institutions, retirees, secondary schools, faculty, industry, the unemployed, the undereducated?

In answering the above questions, trustees should recognize the value that can accrue to the board and college through the contributions made by minority board members and representatives from other groups. For example, minority board members can provide a valuable perspective in interpreting the college to the community and the community to the college. In addition, a governing board with diverse members sends a message to the community that the board is committed to diversity and inclusiveness. Through the board's commitment to diversity, individuals from minority and under-represented groups can serve as role models to students and other community residents.

As indicated throughout this chapter, movement toward diversity on boards is occurring. Between 1969 and 1995, the percentage of women on boards increased from 15% to 33% and the percentage of minority trustees increased from 2% to 13% (Rauh, 1969; CTS). Although these numbers reflect neither the student body nor the population at large, the commitment to representation of diverse groups in community colleges at the board level can be seen by the trends of community college trustee selection. Trends in the kinds of individuals who serve on community college boards is addressed throughout much of this book. The perspectives of trustees and presidents regarding community representation will be dealt with in more detail in chapter 5.

The Trustee- President Team

The trustee-president team is of primary importance to the effective functioning of the community college. More than any other segment of the college community, this team is responsible for what happens at the college.

Essentially everyone familiar with community college governance acknowledges the governing board's role as policymaker and the president's role as policy implementer. But the trustee-president team's influence extends well beyond policies, procedures, and administrative memoranda, for this team influences and shapes the college's image, the campus climate and culture, and the institutional mission.

While all members of the college community and the larger community may not always know precisely what is happening on campus, they certainly can discern if things are going well or poorly. If the trustee-president team is functioning effectively, members of the college community and, to a lesser degree, members of the community sense it; if things are in disarray or if conflict exists between the board and the president, this situation is also sensed.

In commenting on the trustee-president relationship, one community college trustee notes, "I have a unique and exciting opportunity to work with a very visionary board, president, and administration" (TS). Another observes,

"During my tenure we had to select a president; this is the most important function of the board. We were more than fortunate in our choice" (TS). Another trustee notes, "We have an excellent relationship with our president and administration, and I believe there is a shared confidence and trust between us" (TS).

Presidents also understand the value of having good relations with their board, for most realize that "an effective board enhances the president's effectiveness to move the institution in a positive and progressive way" (PS). Another community college president believes that "the board's effectiveness is critical to the effectiveness of the president. [Trustees] are the eyes and ears of the college in the community. They clearly understand and demonstrate the distinction between policy and administration" (PS).

If the relationship between the board and the president is not positive, the impact on the college can be both dramatic and harmful. One community college president laments that at his college:

> the present board has never established a partnership with the president in support of the college. This puts the president and his administration in an adversarial relationship with the board. This has had a very negative impact upon the public relations efforts of the college. The key effect of this type of board-president relationship is its impact upon the credibility of the institution (PS).

Although this president understands the importance of the trustee-president relationship, it is clear that in this case the relationship is not an ideal one.

The presidents responding to the presidential survey agreed that an effective board can improve the president's performance. Working as a team was prominent among the ways presidents feel that trustees and presidents can enhance the effectiveness of trustees, presidents, and the college. The following quotes are from presidents responding to a survey question on the importance of board-president relations:

The president and board should work as a team. When part of the team is ineffective, the entire team suffers.

Because the board and the president are partners in governing the college and in determining the future direction of the institution, both must be effective if they are to reach their combined potential.

The board-president relationship is the most important factor in the success of the college. Acceptable levels of excellence can never be reached if disharmony exists between the board and the president.

A great board can make a mediocre president very effective. A poorly performing board can make an excellent president ineffective.

Since we're a team—a seamless unit—one's success or failure belongs to us all.

There needs to be a symbiotic relationship between the board and the president. A president cannot be effective without an effective board nor can a board be effective without an effective president.

One president distills the board-president relationship to its most basic level by noting that "one feeds off the other."

Similarly, trustees value teamwork. Working as a team with other trustees and with the president ranks high on the list of rewards that trustees identified from serving on the board. The following quotes from trustees responding to a survey question on the satisfactions of serving on the board highlight further the importance trustees place on the trustee-president team.

The pleasure [of serving on the board] comes from being a member of a winning team, the prize being the empowerment of people to lead a productive life.

It is rewarding to be a part of selecting the best, most qualified president for our college . . . and working with this person to make this college the best it can possibly be.

I am blessed with the opportunity to serve on a board that, with the president, is a team whose members respect and like one another.

It is great to see changes in direction [at the college] when the board and president work together.

I find it very rewarding working with a talented, professional president.

Watching the college grow and prosper because of good leadership from the president and the board is very rewarding.

What I find rewarding is working with a president who has done some very innovative and creative things that benefit our whole educational system.

To see the president and board working together to accomplish the college's mission is rewarding.

Working as a team member to advance the interests of the college is very rewarding.

Working in harmony to see our institution meet its goals and educate our people is very rewarding.

Our current board is great. Our president is great. We trust each other.

The teamwork of the total board and the administration is rewarding.

How, then, do trustees and presidents go about the task of building their team?

Building the Team

Building the trustee-president team can be an arduous task, requiring time, patience, understanding, respect, energy, and commitment on the part of both trustees and presidents. The first step in building the team is bringing the players together. This step is clearly the responsibility of the governing board, for it is the board that selects the president.

Ask almost anyone familiar with the role of the community college governing board to name one of the most important tasks of the board, and the answer will likely be that it is to select the college president. Selecting a president is important, in part, because the great majority of trustees adhere to the practice of making policy and having the president carry out that policy. By placing the day-to-day operation of the college in the hands of the president, trustees expect the president to foster (and in some cases to create) and maintain a positive image for the college, thereby creating a positive image for the board as well. The other side of the coin is that if the president is ineffective, the college's image suffers, as does the image of the board that has retained the ineffective president. Moreover, the selection of a president is viewed as a long-term commitment by the board, with the president's tenure often extending beyond an individual trustee's term on the board. It is little wonder, then, that trustees view the selection of the president as one of their most important undertakings.

Whereas creating and maintaining a positive image for a college is an evolutionary process that must be evaluated regularly over a period of time, there are other more immediate reasons why trustees select a president carefully. It is a decision that depends upon trust, mutual support, and compatibility.

Information and Influence. Almost 93% of the trustees state that they rely on the president and the president's staff for most of the information they receive about the college (CTS). As will be discussed below, trustees feel they receive adequate information from presidents, and the presidents feel that it is important to provide the board with adequate information; this information is the basis on which many board decisions are made. Although it is not unusual for the governing board of an organization or institution to rely upon its chief executive officer for information, this reliance means that the board trusts the president to provide adequate information on the organization and to provide it in a timely fashion.

Information provided to the board by the president is the source of much of the influence the president exerts with the board. Indeed, over 86% of the trustees state that the president and staff are the greatest source of influence on the board's decisions. This percentage contrasts with the 6% of trustees who state that the board chair has the greatest influence on the board's decisions (CTS). As one trustee notes in an interview, "You have to have a good relationship with your president and he with his staff, and you have to make sure he knows what you want in order to get the information you need to make a good decision. You've got to . . . rely on him to make sure that he gives you all of the information." This same trustee holds out a word of caution. "The president is in a peculiar position to be able to manipulate the board . . . by the information and the recommendations made by him and his staff. The board has to make sure that it agrees with what the president wants to do and where he wants to take the situation." Understanding where the president wants to take the college requires that the board have adequate information on which to base its decisions, information usually provided by the president.

Presidents are also sensitive to the need to provide adequate information to trustees. As one president is fond of saying, "Uninformed boards vote 'No'." Or, as another president observes, "An unprepared board cannot assess proposals . . . and is unclear as to the most appropriate action. A well-informed, non-confrontational board makes the job [of president] *almost* easy" (PS). Another president believes that "a well-informed board is critical to the success of a college and of a president" (PS). How adequate is the information provided to trustees by the president?

Almost 55% of the responding trustees state that the president provides them with sufficient information to make informed decisions all of the time. Over 39% state that the information is sufficient most of the time. The remaining 6% feel that the information is sufficient some of the time (4.6%) or only occasionally (1.4%)(CTS). Certainly the high percentage of trustees who are satisfied with the information provided by the president implies that presidents work hard to keep their boards informed and that boards are pleased with the information they receive.

Adhering to boundaries. No principle is more revered in the annals of higher education governance than the proclamation that boards make policies and presidents carry them out. Trustees and presidents were asked about their perceptions of how boards adhere to the boundary between policy and administration.

Over 32% of the trustees responding to the survey stated that they adhere to the boundaries between policy and administration all of the time. Another 61% stated that they adhere to the boundaries most of the time. Approximately 6% state that they adhere to the boundaries some of the time. Less than 1% of the trustees feel that they adhere to the boundaries only occasionally (CTS).

Presidents also feel that trustees adhere to the boundary between policy and administration, with over 28% stating that trustees adhere to the boundary all of the time and another 59% stating that they adhere to the boundary most of the time. Over 10% of the presidents feel that trustees adhere to the boundary some of the time and 2% feel that the boundary is adhered to only occasionally (PS).

The trustees' willingness to respect the boundary between policy and administration appears to be relatively high when one considers that it is often indistinct, making it difficult at times to tell what is policy and what is administration. Moreover, it is a rare governing board that has not at one time or another had members who wanted to get involved in the day-to-day affairs of the college. That over 87% of the presidents perceive trustees as respecting the boundary between policy and administration all or most of the time speaks well of how trustees (as perceived by presidents) fulfill their role as policymakers. Nevertheless, it behooves all trustees to remind themselves occasionally that their role is to make policy, not administer the college.

Delegation of Authority. Another way of looking at boundaries between the board and the president is to ask trustees and presidents if they perceive the president as having sufficient authority to administer the college effectively and efficiently. Almost 76% of the trustees feel that governing boards give presidents enough authority to administer the college all of the time. Over 23% feel that sufficient authority to administer the college is granted most of the time (CTS). There is little doubt, then, that the trustees responding to the question (602 responded) feel that governing boards grant presidents adequate authority to administer the college all or most of the time. But how do presidents perceive the adequacy of the authority granted to them by the governing board? Over 96% of the presidents responding to the question (294 responded) feel that they are granted sufficient authority by the governing board all or most of the time to administer the college effectively and efficiently (PS).

Trustees' views of presidents may be influenced somewhat by their own identification with the president's role, perhaps even at times wondering what it would be like to be the president rather than a trustee. Trustees were asked, if they were choosing their career over again, whether the community college presidency would be among their first two or three choices. Over 600 trustees responded to the survey question, with 7.5% stating that they would consider the presidency among their first career choices, and another 26% stated that they might consider the presidency among their first choices (CTS). Whether identifying with the president's role influences trustees' perceptions of that role is pure speculation. On the other hand, knowing that over 33% of the trustees would or might consider the presidency as a career choice seems to be a good introduction to the discussion on how trustees and presidents view each other.

Trustees' and Presidents' Views of Each Other

When approached about participating in this study, one president remarked that he had never heard of presidents being asked by someone doing a study on the governing board to comment on its role. Although this president may be overstating the case, it is true that few studies examine the board's role from the president's perspective. To ask presidents for their perspective on the role of the board seemed logical, for the president is often in an excellent position to assess the board's effectiveness. For example, the above section on how trustees and presidents perceive the authority granted to presidents to administer the college would be less enlightening were the views of presidents not included. On the other hand, because the president works for the board, some presidents might feel it would be presumptuous to evaluate their boss, although many organizations, including community colleges, have avenues through which presidents are evaluated by people who either directly or indirectly work for them. In any event, in an attempt to understand the trustees' role more thoroughly, presidents were asked to comment on the performance and role of their board.

Do presidents view their role as a conduit for information to the board in the same light as trustees do? The answer is a resounding "yes": over 95% of the presidents responding to the survey state that trustees receive most of the information on the college from presidents and their staffs. Only 0.7% state that the information comes from the board chair (PS). These figures compare favorably with the 93% of the trustees who state that they receive most of their information from the president and the 0.8% who receive it from the board chair (CTS).

Presidents also perceive themselves as the greatest source of influence on board decisions, but not to the degree that trustees perceive the president's influence. Almost 79% of the presidents rate themselves as having the greatest influence on the board's decisions (PS), whereas almost 87% of the trustees rate the presidents as being the most influential (CTS). Not surprisingly, perhaps, presidents view the board chair's influence on decisions as being greater than do trustees, with almost 13% of the presidents ranking the chair as exerting the greatest influence on the board's decisions whereas less than 6% of the trustees rank the chair's influence as the greatest (PS; CTS).

Views on the Relationship. Trustees not only employ presidents, they are also concerned with the success of the president once he or she is employed. Indeed, over 97% of the 608 trustees responding to the survey questions on the subject view assessment of the president as an integral part of the board's responsibilities (CTS). In turn, presidents realize that their performance is related to the board's performance. As one president notes, "An effective board enhances the president's effectiveness in moving the institution in a positive and progressive way. Trustees understand the mission. The motivation [provided by] an effective board may provide more positive results than can be measured" (PS).

Trustees were asked two questions on the survey regarding views on trustee-president success. First, they were asked if they hold the success of the president as a top priority. Second, they were asked if the president holds the success of the board as a top priority.

Forty-seven percent of the 609 trustees responding to the survey question about the priority of presidential success stated that they always hold the success of the president to be a top priority. Almost 45% stated that they hold the success of the president to be a top priority most of the time. The remaining trustees hold the success of the president to be important only some of the time (6.7%) or almost never (1.6%)(CTS). Trustees realize that their success is important to presidents. Indeed, 49% of the 602 trustees answering the question regarding how presidents view the success of trustees believe that presidents always hold the success of the board as a top priority. Over 40% feel that the success of the board is a priority for presidents most of the time. The remaining trustees feel that presidents view their success as important only some of the time (7.3%) or almost never (3.2%)(CTS).

Why would any board or president not view the success of the other as a top priority all of the time? The answers to this question vary depending upon the institution, the board, and the president. Most answers likely center around the human element of the trustee-president relationship. As is true with any ongoing relationship, whether it be spouses, employee-supervisor, or trustee-president, the honeymoon often ends, or at least the passions cool. Boards change. New trustees, who did not select the current president, have not invested the time, resources, energy, or personal reputation in the selection process. Thus, new members might not have the same degree of interest in the president's success as those who made the selection. People become disillusioned with relationships; dissatisfaction sets in. They also become bored. In some cases they become angry; in other cases someone's failure might be another person's gain. For example, rare indeed is the president who, at one time or another, has not felt that the board might be better served if a "certain trustee" would leave the board. The same "certain trustee" would probably like to see a new president, explaining in part why all trustees do not hold the president's success to be a high priority. It is important that trustees and presidents remember that their relationship rests upon human values, attitudes, and prejudices as well as upon performance.

Trust and Mutual Support

The cornerstone of most lasting and successful relationships is trust and mutual support. Certainly trust and support are key ingredients of the trustee-president relationship. Two interview questions and two survey questions were devoted to examining the level of trust and mutual support that exists between the board and the president. The assumption underlying the questions was perhaps an obvious one: trustees believe they must have a president they can trust and support; in turn, presidents feel they must be able to trust and support their board. Without mutual trust and support, the trustee-president team cannot function effectively. Recognizing that in relationships such as wife-husband, parent-child, lawyer-client, doctor-patient, minister-parishioner, and numerous others, maintaining trust and support is a delicate balancing act requiring much skill, commitment, and hard work on the part of each party, the trustees and presidents interviewed were asked what they could do to build and maintain a high level of trust and support between the board and the president. As several of those interviewed noted, trust and mutual support must travel a two-way street: to be effective in building and maintaining a college climate that is conducive to achieving the college's mission, trustees and presidents must know that they can trust each other and depend upon each other for support.

If either the board or the president loses the trust or support of the other, the relationship and the college are likely to be heading for trouble. What, then, can be done to maintain and enhance that trust and support? The following comments from trustees and presidents provide answers to the question.

Building and Maintaining Trust: The Trustee's Perspective. Trustees were asked how they would rate the mutual trust and support between the board and the president. Almost 73% of the trustees rated the trust between the board and the president as very strong. Another 21% rated it as somewhat strong. Mutual support between the board and president was also ranked high, with over 75% of the trustees rating it as very strong and over 20% rating it as somewhat strong (CTS).

In building trust, honesty is the best policy as far as trustees are concerned. In the interviews, every trustee noted in one way or another that board members and the president must be absolutely honest with one another, communicating their feelings candidly and openly. As one trustee puts it,

> First, you have to be open with one another and keep each other informed. We believe that you shouldn't surprise one another; the president shouldn't surprise the board and the board shouldn't surprise the president. If we are informed, we can be more trusting and supportive. The president knows he can trust the board because members will bring things up when there is a problem. We

know he is going to keep us informed, and if we don't have enough information or are not comfortable with it, we will find out more before we proceed with the decision.

Trustees feel that in trustee-president relations "the best surprise is no surprise," as the old Holiday Inn ad used to say. Indeed, a number of trustees noted that they did not ever want to be surprised by the president. "I think the first rule is no surprises," surmises one trustee. Another trustee believes that the board should never surprise the president by catching her or him off guard. One board chair notes, "I have a standard rule with our president: there are no surprises." In addition, the chair notes that "the president builds trust and support by having knowledge and by performance. If he performs well, then he is going to build more trust and support from board members." This chair would also want to know what the people the president works with daily, such as faculty, think of him. Do they trust and support him?

Another board member believes that the most important thing in building support and trust is for the board to be candid with the president. "If you feel he is doing the right thing, let him know. If you do not think he is taking the right direction, you have to be open with the president and not grumble among yourselves as trustees. You've got to play it by the book and be honest and forthright like any other relationship."

The president must always keep the board informed if he or she is to maintain trust and support. "I think knowing what is going on builds trust between the board and president . . . to allow feedback from both sides of the table to improve whatever needs to be improved, so that the working relationship blossoms rather than deteriorates" is how one trustee perceives the relationship.

Trust and support, according to one trustee, demands "constant dialogue and reaffirmation of the board's position when needed. This is paramount to a good relationship between the president, the board, and the board chair."

As most trustees and presidents realize, building trust and support are not always free from conflict. As one trustee notes, "Disagreeing [with the president] on a valid basis, not because you are developing an agenda of your own, but having the sort of freedom where you speak up and say, 'have you considered thus and so, have you considered the implications, and so forth' [is important in the relationship]." This trustee also feels it is important that the president have confidence in trustees' abilities to promote the college, including serving as a spokesperson with political leaders.

One trustee warns that it is dangerous for trustees and presidents to become involved in each other's personal affairs. Although he notes that the problem of involvement in personal matters has never existed on his campus, he nevertheless asserts that he does not think "presidents should—and I've learned this from talking with presidents at ACCT meetings—get involved with the board outside of running the college; that is, don't get involved with a board member's personal problems."

This section concludes with a quote that speaks to a number of the points made by other trustees. One trustee comments:

> I think trustees can establish clear expectations because [a relationship of trust and support] is a two-way street. That way the presi-

dent knows what is expected of him or her. If board members are clear in communicating expectations and performance goals, they can feel confident in their judgment later. I guess confidence in the person's integrity is another thing that is intangible and hard to get a grip on, but just by experiencing that individual over time, within six months you know. I would think any board member who is paying attention ought to have a sense of, "Does this president tell me what I need to know?" Does the president tell me things I need to know in ways that are very honest and not couching things or putting a slant on them that would be favorable so he can hide things we might not be pleased to hear? I want to know how the president behaves in a crisis situation. Would he or she put his or her interests above the interest of the institution?

Building and Maintaining Trust: The President's Perspective

How do presidents view trust and mutual support between trustees and presidents? As was the case with trustees, the presidential survey asked presidents how they would rate the mutual support between the board and the president. Presidents, like trustees, feel that mutual trust and support are important. Indeed, almost 77% of the presidents rated the trust between the board and president as being very strong, and another 18% rated trust as being somewhat strong. Seventy-five percent of the presidents ranked the mutual support between the board and president as being very strong and 19% ranked it as somewhat strong (PS). The presidents who were interviewed were asked what they could do to build and maintain trust.

In reviewing the presidents' responses to the interview question on trust, one is reminded that there are three things to consider when buying a home:

location, location, location. In the case of building trust between the board and the president, the three things to consider are communication, communication, communication. All of the presidents interviewed believe that the most important way of building trust is to have clear lines of communication between the board and the president. "I think you have to be very open with your board members, and I don't think you should ever hold anything back. I think you have to present them the good and the bad at all times." Another president echoes a theme that ran throughout the interviews with both presidents and trustees: "Don't surprise the board." He continues, "I think trust is built on character and general good faith and good will in people, and I think you have to expose your frailties as well as your strengths to the board." One president feels that trust is the "linchpin" in relations between the board and the president. To assure that the linchpin stays in place, "the integrity of the president must be constantly maintained, and the board must believe that anything it hears from him must be the truth and nothing but the truth." Another president warns against surprising the board. As he notes, "the eleventh commandment of board-presidential relations is thou shalt not surprise the board." The key to avoiding surprises is, he feels, open communication between the president and the board.

One president, whose college's service region covers 12,000 square miles, makes it a point to meet with every board member every month. "We talk about next month's agenda and concerns they might have about the agenda. In those meetings I tell about all of the little dragons that are out there that could bite us, and I don't want our trustees to be caught unaware when those things bite." Another president believes that in addition to providing the board with information, he must be accessible. He feels that retreats help build trust between the board and the president. Another president notes that if the board is to trust her, she must see that board members have all of the information they need to make decisions. She also believes that it is important to "act with trust and integrity so you never find yourself in a situation where you have to explain why people didn't have the information or had inaccurate information."

One president cautions against presidents taking the board for granted. "I have observed some presidents and boards where presidents, through whatever process, feel that they do not really report to the board; I think that's deadly to developing trust." Consistency is important in building trust, according to one president: "The president needs to be the same with trustees as he is with faculty and community members—with everyone—so people are all hearing the same story."

Accessibility and Responsiveness. Both trustees and presidents clearly believe that effective communication improves the trust and mutual support between the president and the board. If effective communication is to take place, trustees and presidents must be accessible and responsive to each other. Trustees were asked how accessible the president is to individual trustees. Almost 90% of the trustees perceive the president to be available to trustees daily. Less than 1% feel that the president is available to individual trustees only before or after a board meeting or through the board chair (CTS). Almost all board chairs (96%) perceive the president to be accessible to them on a daily basis (CS).

Presidents perceive themselves to be available to individual trustees as needed, with over 87% stating that they are available daily versus the less than 1%

stating that they were available before or after board meetings or through the board chair. Over 90% of the presidents perceive themselves to be available to the board chair daily (PS).

Presidents are not only available to their board chairs; they meet with the chairs regularly. Almost 29% of the presidents responding to the survey state that they meet with their board chairs once a week; almost 34% of the presidents meet with their chair every two weeks; 27% of the presidents meet with the chair once a month, and approximately 10% of the presidents state that meetings with board chairs occur less often than once a month (PS). The channel of communication between the board chair and the president is seemingly open and, based upon the frequency of meeting between the chair and president, used often.

In asking themselves about the availability of the president daily, trustees might want to be sensitive to the fact that most presidents must be available to eight or more trustees, whereas an individual trustee may see the availability of the president on a one-to-one basis. Also, based upon the frequency of the meetings between the chair of the board and the president, it is unlikely that individual trustees need to meet with the president often, assuming the full board shares in the products of the chair-president meetings, when appropriate. In any event, the availability of the president to individual trustees is not viewed as a problem by either trustees or presidents.

So presidents are available to trustees. But are presidents perceived by trustees to be responsive when approached by trustees? The answer is "yes." Almost 86% of the 613 trustees answering the question perceive the president to be very responsive; almost 13% perceive the president to be somewhat responsive to the board (CTS).

Presidents were asked to rate their responsiveness to the governing board. Not surprisingly, considering that presidents serve at the pleasure of the board, over 95% of the presidents perceive themselves to be very responsive to the board; not one of the 295 presidents responding to the survey question perceive themselves to be unresponsive when the board comes calling (PS).

Keeping in mind that responsiveness must be a two-way street if effective communication is to take place, trustees were asked how they would rate the board's responsiveness to the president. Almost 91% of the trustees believe that they are very responsive to the president; over 8% perceive themselves to be somewhat responsive (CTS). Presidents also perceive the governing board to be very responsive, with over 84% of the presidents perceiving the board to be very responsive to the president. Not one of the 294 presidents responding to the survey perceives the board to be unresponsive to presidents (PS).

Viewed from the perspectives of both trustees and presidents, the conclusion is that presidents are available to trustees when needed and both governing boards and presidents respond to each others' needs. Availability and responsiveness should assist communication and build trust between governing boards and presidents.

When Trust Breaks Down

Both trustees and presidents were asked in interviews what they would do if they did not trust the information being provided by the board or president. While both trustees and presidents felt that it would be very unusual to receive information they did not trust, as reported above, they nevertheless felt that should the situation occur, it should be dealt with immediately.

Trustees. Should he not trust the information received from the president, one trustee stated that he would seek more information and, if not satisfied, would take the issue to the board chair. Another trustee calls this question "a tough one." He would evaluate the situation and "go to my chair who has direct contact with the president and hope that he would either clear up the problem or raise it with the whole board." Another trustee would bring the issue before the board in executive session. He would then offer the president "an opportunity to review his position and his information and take action from that point." Another trustee believes, "First of all, you have to operate through the chairperson. What this means is that no matter how sticky an issue might be, you are open and honest with the president. You cannot circumvent the president and the president cannot circumvent the board chair."

Another trustee would try to obtain information "without embarrassing the president." Then, "If I found the president had made a mistake, I would help the president rectify that mistake. If the president were deliberately deceiving the board, I would meet with the board and take some corrective action." Another trustee's response is to pick the right person to start with. But if that does not work, she feels that "you can't really tinker around with that one too much, for if you find somebody you mistrust, I think that can't be fixed."

Another trustee would react as follows: "First of all, I would speak with my board chair; and if I were not satisfied, I would probably speak to other members of the board and say that I have a lack of trust in the college president. Then I feel it is the board, as a whole, that must decide what the next steps would be." Another trustee would express her feelings to the chair and see if other trustees shared her view. One trustee would "press for more information. At times I find it is justified to circumvent the president totally and go straight to the source of the information." She would, however, involve other trustees in her search for information.

One board chair states that if he did not trust the information he would find the correct information. "Then I would call it to the president's attention and get his answer on why it is wrong. Then we'd have a discussion as to why he was giving me wrong information." Yet another trustee would discuss his feeling with the board chair, and "then if other people on the board felt the same way, I think you need to broach the subject with the president and have a real heart-to-heart with the president."

To summarize, all of the trustees interviewed would involve the entire board in confronting the issue of a lack of trust in information provided by the president. Most trustees would work through the board chair in resolving the issue. All trustees implied strongly that they would view the breakdown in trust between the board and the president as a major issue and one that would have to be dealt with openly, directly, and quickly. Their approach would seem to be one that would build trust among the members of the board and enhance their ability to handle difficult situations.

Presidents. Those presidents interviewed were asked how they would react if they did not trust the information given to them by the board chair. Some of their comments and solutions follow.

> I think I would probably find an opportunity to talk with the chair on the side and not in the presence of the other board members. I would want to be sure that I understand exactly what is being said and that he understands what I am saying to be sure that there is [a reason] for mistrust. If it goes beyond that, I would probably take it to the next step and try to bring it before one of the board's committees and talk openly about this topic so that it is put on the table and other board members understand what is going on.

Another president responded as follows: "Oh my gosh, I might let it go to see if I'm making wrong assessments. But if it were very evident that the representations weren't ethical and fair, I would have to confront the individual. I would do this individually before I would confront him in the presence of the rest of the board." He was then asked what he would do if he did not get a resolution. "I'd probably have to consider whether I wanted to stay there. Some jobs aren't worth having under the wrong conditions."

Another veteran president admits that the issue is, "well, a rough one." His advice illustrates why he has been successful in three different presidencies. He would have a meeting with the board chair, and if he did not get satisfactory answers, he would go to the full board and,

> let them see where the discrepancy is as opposed to going in and telling them your chair is doing a, b, c, d, and e. You don't want to

be in a position where you are accusing either the chair or the other board members of being dishonest, not trustworthy, or whatever the case might be. Let them [the other board members] come to that conclusion on the basis of the facts that you present to them.

While most of the presidents interviewed stated that they had never had to face a situation where they did not trust information given to them by the board chair, one president speaks from recent experience. He states:

Actually I have had to face the situation and it puts you in a bind, puts you in a position where you are pretty much stymied. You have to use your instincts in terms of what you do with that information. One of the things that is important is that the president needs to protect the chair regardless of the relationship and the fact that the board chair may not be shooting straight. I would be careful not to take erroneous information and spread it around in a way that embarrasses the chair. That's a tough one. I'm not sure there is a way around it.

The president was asked if he confronted the board chair. "Yes, and his reaction was pretty much a denial." He was then asked what he did. He responded, "Just pretty much had to accept that." It is interesting to note that the president left his position to assume another presidency shortly after the interview was completed.

Similarly, another president states that, although he has never had to face a situation where he did not trust the information given to him by the chair, should it occur, he would go to the board chair but approach the subject gingerly. "I would deal with it somewhat directly, but in a very politic way, suggesting that perhaps there are other views and maybe those other views were overlooked." One president sees it as follows: "I think if I couldn't trust a board chair, I might try to talk with other board members about changing the board chair. I might be willing to wait a year to see if we couldn't get another chair elected; but if we couldn't, I would resign."

In a similar fashion, another president would confront the board chair directly. If no solution were arrived at, "I would either ask him to consider resigning and letting someone else take the role or I would advise him that if he is unwilling to do that, then I would start looking for another job." Finally, one president would go directly to the chair if he did not trust the information he was receiving from the chair. If the issue were not resolved, he "would probably go to the college attorney who works for the college and the board. Also, I would probably go to a board member that I have a good trusting relationship with."

As with trustees, presidents would confront the issue of mistrust head on, in most cases going to the board chair first and the full board next, assuming it was necessary. An interesting contrast between the board and presidents emerged that reinforces rule number one about board-presidential relations: if an issue is not resolved, boards can remove presidents. Presidents, on the other hand, cannot remove trustees. If they cannot resolve the issue, presidents can choose to resign.

Summary

This chapter has examined that critical component of the college's governing structure, the trustee-president team. From the survey questions and the interviews, it is clear that both trustees and presidents believe that the board-president relationship is a symbiotic one. The attitude, in general, is that what is good for the president is good for the board and what is good for the board is good for the president, and most important, what is good for both is good for the college. After all, the good of the college is what every trustee and president must work for. The best way for trustees and presidents to raise the college to its highest level of excellence is to work as a team, for rarely can a community college reach its full potential unless the board and the president function as a team.

Trustees

on the

Job

America is a nation of volunteers.
Indeed, one of the defining characteristics
of America's brand of democracy is its emphasis on volunteerism as an avenue for fulfilling one's civic duties.

Citizen-soldier George Washington set the stage when he volunteered to lead
the Colonial army against the British. The tradition of volunteerism continues today in its many forms in every community in the nation. An important
avenue through which some of the nation's citizens fulfill their civic duty is by
volunteering their time, knowledge, experience, energy, and resources to serve
on the governing boards of the nation's community colleges.

Service on a community college governing board is limited to a few select
individuals, however. Why? First, the number of positions is limited. (The
number of trustees on a board ranges from five to 30, with the average
between eight and nine, and seven as the most common number.) Second,
although serving on the board is a voluntary activity, trustees must be either
appointed or elected before they can serve. Third, most trustees earn the
right to serve on the board through previous public service, influence,
accomplishments, or political connections.

Once an individual is selected to serve on the board, the message to the
community is that the individual is an important member of the community who has something to contribute to its welfare. For example, as discussed in chapter 2 of this book, the great majority of community college

trustees are well-educated, affluent, successful people. What, then, do trustees do once they are selected to serve on the board? How much time do they devote to serving? Is serving as a trustee stressful? Do trustees attend board meetings regularly, and are they prepared for the meetings they attend? How do trustees communicate with faculty? These and other questions will be explored in this chapter.

Trustees and presidents were asked what trustees do once they are selected to serve. The following discussion is based upon their responses.

Allocation of Effort and Time

Using a scale of 1 to 10, with 1 representing *no effort* and 10 representing *almost all of the trustee's effort,* trustees were asked to rate the overall amount of effort they expend on various activities that fall within the board's purview. The purpose of using the rating scale was not to measure hours spent on board activities (the next section deals with hours) but to obtain trustees' perceptions of the relative importance of board activities. Figure 4.1 shows the relative rankings of all trustees responding to the survey.

Although not shown in the figure, veteran trustees have learned that the amount of effort expended on any given activity varies from one college to another and from one time to another. For example, if the college has a budget crisis, more time and effort will be required in the areas of budget and financial management than would be required during normal times. The rankings are valuable, nevertheless, in understanding what trustees see as requiring most of their effort.

Hours Spent on College Matters. In addition to asking trustees how they expended their efforts, the survey asked them how much time they spent on

Figure 4.1　Amount of effort spent on board activities

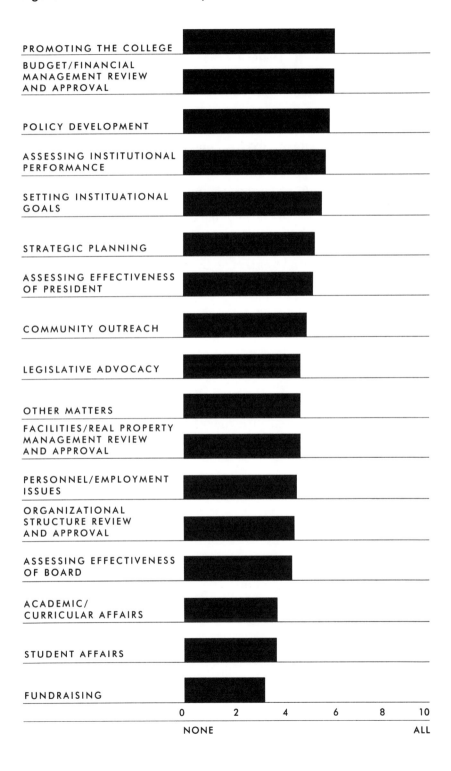

PROMOTING THE COLLEGE					
BUDGET/FINANCIAL MANAGEMENT REVIEW AND APPROVAL					
POLICY DEVELOPMENT					
ASSESSING INSTITUTIONAL PERFORMANCE					
SETTING INSTITUATIONAL GOALS					
STRATEGIC PLANNING					
ASSESSING EFFECTIVENESS OF PRESIDENT					
COMMUNITY OUTREACH					
LEGISLATIVE ADVOCACY					
OTHER MATTERS					
FACILITIES/REAL PROPERTY MANAGEMENT REVIEW AND APPROVAL					
PERSONNEL/EMPLOYMENT ISSUES					
ORGANIZATIONAL STRUCTURE REVIEW AND APPROVAL					
ASSESSING EFFECTIVENESS OF BOARD					
ACADEMIC/ CURRICULAR AFFAIRS					
STUDENT AFFAIRS					
FUNDRAISING					
	0	2	4	6	8	10
	NONE					ALL

board matters each week. Figure 4.2 shown below depicts the time board members spend on college activities each week.

The mean number of hours spent on board matters by chairs and non-chairs as a group is approximately five hours per week. Approximately 12% of trustees state that they spend up to one hour per week on board matters. Twenty-four trustees (6.5%) out of the 581 responding to the question estimated that they spend up to 15 or more hours per week on board matters, with one trustee spending up to 50 hours per week. The majority of the trustees (62.5%) spend from two to five hours per week on board matters, and almost 19% spend from six to ten hours per week (CTS). The workload, then, is fairly heavy for a group of volunteers. One trustee observes that "I'm retired, otherwise I could not keep up with the demands of the board."

Chairs and Non-chairs. One would assume that chairs (160 chairs responded to the question) would expend more time on board matters than do trustees as a whole. The following data provide some insights into this assumption.

Over 64% of the chairs spend from one to five hours per week on board matters, and over 26% spend from six to ten hours per week (CS). Of the non-chairs, over 78% spend from one to five hours per week and over 16% spend from six to ten hours per week on board matters (TS). None of the chairs responded that they spent over 20 hours per week on board matters (CS); yet 2.2% of the non-chair trustees stated that they did (TS).

Why does serving as chair of the board not demand more time than serving as a member of the board without the chair's responsibilities? Using the

Figure 4.2 Number of hours per week that trustees spend on board activities

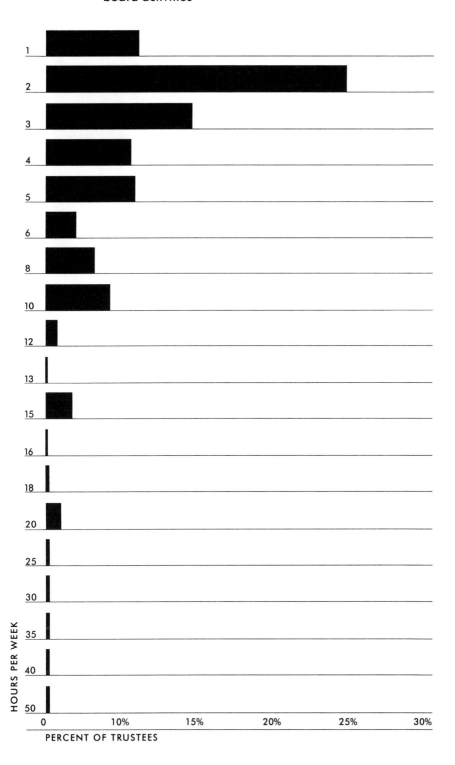

information obtained from the surveys alone, one can only speculate on why this situation is true. One explanation might be that the chair has more experience as a board member and, therefore, is more familiar with the college's policies and procedures and the demands of being a member of the board. For example, less than 5% of the chairs have served on the board for one to two years, and over 36% have served from three to six years (CS). In contrast, 24% of the non-chairs have been on the board from one to two years, and 31% of the non-chairs have been on the board for from three to six years (TS).

Further reducing the time required by the chair might be that he or she has worked with the same president for a number of years and knows what to expect from the president in terms of information, requests, and support. In any event, time spent on college matters should not be taken as an indication of the importance of the chair's position; on many boards, the chair is crucial to the trustee-president team and to the efficient and effective operation of the board.

Stress. Most trustees do not find serving on the community college's governing board a stressful undertaking. For example, among the non-chair trustees, only 4% find board membership to be very stressful; over 34% find it to be moderately stressful; over 61% find that it is not very stressful at all (TS).

Chairs find serving on the board to be somewhat more stressful than do non-chairs. Almost 5% of the chairs find serving to be very stressful; over 46% find it moderately stressful; over 48% of the chairs find service on the board to be not very stressful at all (CS).

Of course, serving as a trustee can be very stressful when a crisis occurs. The stress meter rises rapidly when a president must be dismissed, when a union contract is being negotiated, or when the college has a budget shortfall. In general, however, for most trustees, serving on the board is not very stressful at all and, as will be discussed later, is a pleasant and rewarding way to pay one's "civic rent," as one trustee describes board membership.

Functioning as a Trustee

As discussed in chapter 3, the board-president team is integral to the college's success. Also important is how the board functions as a body. The following perceptions from board members and presidents answer questions regarding the balance of power on the board, trustee workloads, interaction among trustees, preparation for board meetings, and attendance patterns of board members.

Balance of Power. Trustees were asked to describe the balance of power on the board. Does the board chair dominate or lead the board? Do other members dominate? Or, is there an equal balance of power on the board, with no one dominating?

Less than 3% of the trustees perceive the board to be dominated by the chair, whereas almost 38% perceive the chair as leading rather than dominating the board. Over 53% of the trustees feel that there is an equal balance of power on the board, whereas slightly over 6% feel that one or more trustees dominate the board (CTS).

Presidents' perceptions are similar to those of trustees: 3.7% of the presidents perceive that the board is dominated by the chair; almost 49% feel that the chair leads the board but does not dominate the board; 40% perceive the balance of power to be equally balanced between the chair and other trustees; and 7.5% of the presidents perceive that one or more trustees dominate the board (PS).

The perceptions of trustees and presidents indicate that most boards have the balance of power in proper perspective: the board chair provides leadership but does not dominate the board.

Work Responsibilities. Is the balance of power on the board reflected in the amount of work done by trustees? That is, is the workload shared equitably among board members? Almost 60% of the trustees feel that there is equal participation among trustees in doing the work of the board; over 16% feel that a few trustees do most of the work (an active committee structure could lead to this perception); 1.3% perceive the chair as doing most of the work; and almost 23% perceive the president as doing most of the board's work (CTS).

Over 48% of the presidents perceive that the board's workload is shared equally among trustees. Almost 17% perceive that most of the work is done by a few board members; 1.4% perceive that the chair does most of the work; and almost 34% of the presidents perceive the president doing most of the work for the board (PS).

As is true with the balance of power, trustee workload would appear to present most boards with few problems. That presidents perceive themselves as doing more work for the board than trustees perceive to be the case might be due to most trustees not being aware of the many hours that presidents and their staffs devote to answering relatively minor questions raised by trustees. In any event, neither chairs, other trustees, nor presidents seem to bear an inordinate amount of the board's workload.

Interaction Among Board Members. Overwhelmingly, trustees perceive that board members cooperate with each other. (Over 85% of the trustees felt that *cooperation* best described the interaction among board members.) Slightly more than 10% perceived that board members act professionally, even though they may not always get along with each other. Less than 5% of the trustees responding to the survey stated that trustees place more importance on promoting their own interests than they do on cooperating with each other (CTS).

Presidents perceive the interaction among board members in a similar fashion. Almost 82% of the presidents felt that trustees generally cooperate with each other in a professional manner. Twelve percent of the presidents perceive that board members act professionally, although they may not always get along with each other. Slightly over 6% of the presidents perceive trustees as promoting their own interests over cooperating with each other (PS).

Clearly trustees and presidents perceive the board to be a cohesive group, with most trustees cooperating with each other. The relatively small number of trustees perceived by trustees and presidents to promote their own interests indicates that self-interest is not a major problem for most community college governing board members.

Preparing for Board Meetings. Rare is the board chair or president who has not, at one time or another, feared that some members of the board would arrive at an important board meeting unprepared to debate an important issue. The fear is magnified if the meeting has caught the eye of the media. Does the fear have a base in reality? Yes, somewhat. Eighty-six percent of the trustees perceive that all or most trustees arrive at board meetings fully prepared for the meeting; the remaining trustees (14%) perceive that some trustees are adequately prepared for board meetings only some of the time (CTS).

Eighty percent of the presidents perceive that all or most trustees are fully prepared for board meetings, and the remainder (20%) feel that only some of the trustees are adequately prepared for board meetings (PS).

Most trustees are busy people, and most community colleges provide an overwhelming amount of information to their boards. Community college boards meet often, with 75% meeting monthly and 10% meeting twice a month (CS). Preparing for a board meeting is a time-consuming task. Based upon the first author's experiences and what he has learned from talking with presidents and trustees, most board chairs and presidents assure that members of the board are adequately prepared when an important issue is to be brought before the board. In reality, most boards work through important issues in committee before bringing them to the full board.

Attendance at Board Meetings. Perhaps an even greater fear for trustees and presidents than whether trustees will arrive at a board meeting unprepared is the fear that they will not arrive at all. Based upon the survey results, this fear is unfounded. Almost 99% of the trustees observe that all or most trustees attend board meetings regularly (CTS). Ninety-three percent of presidents perceive that all or most trustees attend meetings regularly (PS). Board attendance does not seem to be a problem, although in practice some boards have that member who manages to miss far too many meetings. Non-attendance at board meetings is rare, with a mere 1.5% of the trustees perceiving attendance at board meetings to be a problem with some trustees and a small percentage (2.7%) of the presidents sharing the trustees' perceptions (CTS; PS).

Orientation of New Board Members. There is no better time to emphasize the importance of attending board meetings and preparing for those meetings than when trustees first join the board. Board chairs were asked if new board members participate in a formal orientation upon becoming a member of their community college's governing board. Of the 171 chairs responding to the survey question, over 69% stated that new board members voluntarily participate in a formal orientation at their college when they join the board; 14% of the chairs stated that a formal orientation for new board members is mandatory. Sixteen percent of the trustees responding to the question stated that new trustees have no formal orientation upon joining the board (CS).

The board chairs were also asked who conducts the formal orientation for new trustees. (The chairs were asked to "circle all that apply" from the choices offered on the survey; therefore, the total equals more than 100%.) Of the 143 chairs responding to the question, 86% stated that the formal orientation is conducted by the president and president's staff; another 47% of the chairs stated that the board chair conducts orientation; 15% state that outside consultants conduct the orientation; and 22% state that other individuals are involved in the orientation for new board members (CS).

Presidents were asked who they believe should be responsible for the orientation of new trustees. Of the 294 presidents responding to the survey question, over 72% believe that the orientation should be conducted by the board chair, president and staff; over 21% stated that they believe the president and staff should conduct the orientation; less than 2% believe that the board chair should do the orientation; and less than 5% believe the orientation should be conducted by others (PS).

Trustees new to the board should be eager to learn as much as they can as quickly as they can about the duties and responsibilities of being a member of the governing board. A formal orientation involving, at a minimum, the board chair, president, and president's staff provides an excellent opportunity to assure that new trustees understand what service on the board entails. Trustees need to ask themselves if this opportunity is being utilized effectively as their boards welcome new members.

Time on Campus. The majority of trustees and presidents perceive the amount of time trustees spend on campus to be appropriate. Almost 65% of the trustees perceive the amount to be proper; over 86% of the presidents have the same perception. A small percentage (1.5%) of the trustees perceive the time they spend on campus to be excessive; less than 1% of the presidents share that perception (CTS; PS).

There is some disagreement between trustees and presidents over how much time trustees *should* spend on campus. Almost 34% of the trustees perceive that they should spend more time on campus than they currently do, whereas only 13% of the presidents believe that trustees should spend more time on campus than they do (CTS; PS).

The difference between how much time trustees feel they should spend on campus versus how much time presidents feel trustees should spend has some logical explanations. For example, trustees may feel guilty if they cannot attend a major campus ceremony or even if they are unable to attend minor campus events to which they are invited. On the other hand, some presidents may fear that if trustees are on campus often, they will be tempted to become involved in too many of the day-to-day activities of the campus, thus crossing the line between policymaking and administration.

Based upon the above data, trustees and presidents are generally in agreement on how boards approach the routine but important tasks and activities associated with board membership. Indeed, the above discussion further documents that trustees and presidents have similar perceptions regarding the governing board's role.

Trustees and Faculty

Dealing with the faculty is seen by most presidents as presidential territory. Yet the board is responsible for the well-being of the total college, which includes the faculty. Trustees take this responsibility seriously. Over 58% of the trustees responding to the survey state that they give serious consideration to faculty opinions most of the time; almost 30% state that faculty opinions are considered seriously some of the time; less than 4% rarely consider faculty opinions important (CTS). The challenge for the board is to communicate with faculty without moving into the president's territory.

The challenge goes beyond the boundary between policy and administration discussed in chapter 3, for communicating with the faculty is usually more personal and more emotional than simply making and following policy.

For example, it is difficult for trustees to refuse to talk with faculty about an important issue if a faculty member requests an audience. Of course, talking with faculty about important issues does not mean that trustees take action based upon the discussions. On the other hand, talking directly with the faculty about issues affecting the college versus informal discussions at social events and campus ceremonies may be seen as bypassing the president, as moving into presidential territory, especially if the discussion takes place without the president's knowledge.

Trustees were asked on the survey how faculty communicate with them. Almost 85% of the trustees stated that when faculty communicate with them, it is through the president or with the knowledge of the president. At the other end of the scale, almost 16% of the trustees state that faculty communicate with them directly without the president's knowledge (CTS).

Forty-three percent of the presidents responded that faculty communication with the board occurs through the president. Another 28% state that faculty communication with the board is done with the president's knowledge. The remaining 29% of the presidents feel that faculty communication with the board is direct and without the president's knowledge (PS). The 29% is almost double the 15.4% of the trustees who feel that faculty communicate directly with them without the president's knowledge (CTS), suggesting that presidents and trustees should discuss their perceptions of the avenues of communication between the board and the faculty. Trustees' and presidents' responses to the survey are obviously based upon their perceptions, which in turn grow out of their experiences. Based upon the experience and observations of the first author, it would not be unusual for presidents to perceive some faculty as bypassing the president when communicating with the board. On the other hand, board members would be less likely to perceive that the faculty is coming directly to them and bypassing the president. Each trustee-president team must decide if faculty communicating directly with trustees without the knowledge of the president is a problem. If a problem exists, then it should be resolved through board policy, or at least discussed openly between the board and the president.

The question of how trustees communicate with the faculty and other members of the college community seemed to be an important question warranting further investigation, for how faculty concerns are treated often plays a major role in how the college is governed. Therefore, both trustees and presidents were asked in interviews how they perceive communications between trustees and members of the college community taking place. Their responses to the interview questions confirm how important both trustees and presidents believe the topic of board-faculty communications to be.

Beyond the Statistics

Trustees and Faculty. Some trustees were adamant that all communications with the faculty or any other member of the college community be only through the president. One trustee, when asked how trustees communicate with the faculty replied, "We don't. We do it through the president according to [board] policies." Another trustee, while noting that obviously trustees talk with faculty at college functions such as graduation and awards ceremonies, states, "We do not as trustees do a one-on-one [with the faculty] regarding any board policies or anything having to do with the institution. That's the president's job." One trustee, who notes that formal communication occurs through reports from the faculty and board at board meetings and as a part of the information flow on campus, realizes that informal communication with the faculty must take place. As did several trustees, she distinguishes between formal and informal communication: "We have four separate campuses, so we travel to each of them throughout the year. We are on campus for different functions, so our involvement with faculty on an informal basis is because we are present at events on campus."

Several trustees noted that they tended to keep their doors cracked, if not fully open, for communicating with the faculty. As one notes,

> I very rarely communicate with the college staff, particularly outside of a board meeting. Being a small college, you run into people socially, so you do communicate some, but I think you do it very carefully. You don't do it on the basis of going to the staff on your own either to get information or carry out your own agenda. We have a policy with our board that we don't even ask faculty or administrators to get information for an inquiry unless the majority of the board members feel that the inquiry is significant. So, I'm not saying you can't talk to college personnel, but I think you've got to be very circumspect and make sure you aren't doing it for your personal agenda.

Another board member states, "If I need to contact them [the faculty] personally I will. But otherwise, if it is something in general, I will go through the chancellor." Asked what she would do if a faculty member came to her with a problem, she replied, "You evaluate the problem first. If it is something that is not a personal problem with the chancellor, I would take the problem to the chancellor."

Another trustee, while in general agreement that communication with the faculty should be through the president, illustrates the complexity of communicating with the faculty. Her answer shows how difficult (and for her, impractical at times) it is to communicate with the faculty only through the president. She also explains that board policy may encourage direct contact with the faculty.

As a trustee, I [initiate] virtually no direct communication with the faculty and staff. . . . If a member of the faculty or staff contacts me for some reason, which upon occasion happens (and the same is true of somebody in the community), it depends on the nature of the call. When I was chair, . . . I was requested to attend events on behalf of the board, and if someone called me from the faculty and asked me to do that, I would have no objection whatsoever to just doing it. Now, however, if a faculty member called me and said, "You know, I would really like to discuss something with you, [for] there is something that really bothers me that is going on here," my first response would be to ask, "Have you gone through the appropriate chain of command within the college?" That is really a cautious one. Sometimes you do need to listen when you get a call like that; we were in a position where we had to fire a prior president because of some calls that came like that. That is a real tricky situation because, in that case, we had most of the six deans and a couple of other administrators who placed calls to us. I think it was fairly apparent at that point—because of the respect that we had for those people—that there was something wrong. And at that point, we chose to listen. But most of the time, you do not as a trustee entertain complaint-type calls without referring them on. And certainly if you did have one, I think you would then want to go to the president and say that the call had come.

Do faculty members and trustees have a professional relationship and, in some cases, a legal relationship with each other that removes conversations between faculty and trustees from the realm of citizens communicating with elected officials? One board member feels that he has an obligation as an elected official to communicate directly with those who elected him. (Here a case could be made that elected board members are subject to greater influence from constituents than are appointed trustees, especially if the trustee was elected through the efforts of a special interest group.) He notes, "I just retired after 34 years in a high school classroom, so I know a lot of people from my professional work. They were strong supporters of my campaign, so I knew them politically and personally. When I have questions, I can talk to them as friends, but I try not to do it if it is board business."

While noting that he normally goes through the president when communicating with the faculty, this trustee also notes, "We have a very strong academic senate and a very strong union. As a matter of fact, yesterday I spent two hours with the president of the union discussing mutual concerns. [I was acting] as a trustee because I am an elected official. The public has a right to ask me questions and talk to me in private. I don't have the right to make decisions [for the board]." Although this trustee indicated that he shares whatever information he gathers with other trustees, it would seem that trustee contact with faculty leaders to discuss college issues raises some questions, especially if the discussion takes place without the knowledge of the board chair and president.

Some boards have taken steps to mitigate one-on-one college-related conversations between trustees and members of the college community that bypass the president. One trustee notes that his college has a strict policy regarding communicating with the faculty: "We have a standard communications policy that explicitly spells out the channels of communication from top down and from down up. Every board member is thoroughly versed in that communications policy and understands that if there is any attempt by a faculty member or a member of the staff to communicate directly with the board, these communications are referred to the president."

Whether board policy states how communications with the faculty take place or whether an elected trustee feels an obligation to talk with constituents (including faculty and staff), many of the trustees agree that the responsibility for effective communication between the board and the college community rests primarily with the president. Those trustees interviewed, for the most part, choose to use the president as the conduit through which they communicate with the faculty if that communication is likely to influence or result in actions by the board.

Trustees' Worst Fear

In a previous book, the first author titled one of the chapters "How Long Is Too Long? The Question Presidents and Trustees Fear to Ask" (Vaughan, 1989, p. 46). The "how long is too long" referred to presidential tenure. The reason trustees and presidents fear to ask the question involves the complications that often ensue when one tries to answer it, and especially the complication that occurs if the board's answer is that the incumbent president's tenure has been too long. At times the first author has suggested, somewhat in jest, that the most important decision trustees make is to hire the president, and the second most important decision trustees make is getting rid of their most important decision. The point is, of course, that employing and dismissing a president are both important undertakings, and, in the case of dismissal, often traumatic for community college trustees, the college president, and members of the college community.

Much has been written on employing community college presidents. Rather than going too deeply into this aspect of the board's role and responsibility (some aspects of the employing process are dealt with elsewhere in this book), the authors chose to ask trustees to think about the possibility of having to dismiss a president who is not as effective as the board desires. The following responses give some indication of why trustees move cautiously before dismissing a president they feel is less effective than the board desires. (Chapter 3 discusses how trustees view the importance of the president's success.)

Fear of Legal Action. Seventy-seven percent of the trustees feel that the fear of legal action would carry little weight in their decision to dismiss a president. Nevertheless, twenty-three percent of the trustees noted that the fear of legal action by the president would be important (CTS).

Time and Costs. Seventy-six percent of the trustees feel that cost and time of a presidential search would be relatively unimportant in their decision to dismiss a president. The remaining trustees (24%) stated that the cost and time involved in conducting a presidential search would be an important consideration in their decision to dismiss a president (CTS).

Female Incumbent. Almost 75% of the trustees feel that the incumbent's being a woman would be unimportant in their decision to dismiss a president; slightly over 16% noted that the fact that the president is a woman would be somewhat important. Over 9% of the trustees noted that the incumbent's being a woman would be important in their decision to dismiss a president (CTS).

Minority Incumbent. Seventy-one percent of the trustees feel that the incumbent's being a minority would be unimportant in their decision to dismiss a president; 18% stated that this fact would be somewhat important; and 11% stated that the president's being a minority would be important in their decision to dismiss the president (CTS).

The Effectiveness of the Next President. Over 38% of the trustees noted that the fear that the next president might not be as effective as the current one would be important in their decision to dismiss a president. Twenty-two percent feel it would be somewhat important in their decision, and over 39% of the trustees feel that this fear would not be important at all in their decision to dismiss a president (CTS).

A Lack of Knowledge of the Dismissal Process. Fifty-nine percent of the trustees did not feel that a lack of knowledge about the process of dismissing a president would be an important consideration should they decide to dismiss a president. However, a lack of knowledge would be important to almost 21% of the trustees, and over 20% stated that this would be a somewhat important consideration (CTS).

Fear of a Split Board. As discussed earlier, board cohesiveness is an important consideration for trustees and presidents. Sixty-nine percent of the trustees feel that the fear of a board split on the decision to dismiss a president would be somewhat important (over 23%) or not important (over 45%) to consider. The remaining 31% stated that the fear that a split would occur on the board would be an important consideration should they decide to dismiss a president (CTS).

Approximately nine out of ten trustees felt that the incumbent president's being a woman or a minority would be of little importance when the time came to dismiss the president. The low percentages indicate that trustees evaluate presidents on performance, not on gender, race, or ethnic background. Trustees' responses also suggest that concerns about legal action, the costs and time involved in employing a new president, concerns that the next president would be less effective than the current one, a lack of knowledge about how to dismiss a president, and concerns that dismissing a president would bring about a split on the board would not likely prevent a board from considering dismissing a president. However, the act of dismissing a president is considered serious business.

Policymaking and Delegation

A recurring theme that weaves its way throughout this book is the governing board's role in making policy. This fact is not surprising, for the board's policies influence everything from the college's mission to what programs the college offers. In an attempt to understand how trustees make policy and operate as a board, the trustees were asked several questions regarding policymaking and delegation of authority. Their perceptions are summarized in the following two sections.

Setting the Board Agenda and Making Policy. The trustees interviewed were asked how they go about setting the board agenda and in general how they go about setting policy. One trustee notes that his board places major emphasis on working through committees. The board has two standing committees, one on finance and one on academic affairs. "Every board member has an appointment to one of those communities so a board member has the opportunity to participate in either one of those areas." In addition, the trustee observes, "My philosophy of governance of a public institution is that when you have a particular decision to make, you create a committee; you appoint board members to the committee, or solicit board participation. The committee is given specific instructions to solve the problem and report to the board and the board takes appropriate action. I have found this is one way to keep down controversy because the issues tend to be aired in committee."

One trustee noted that his board has a policy committee that reviews all existing policies and makes a decision as to whether the policies need to be updated. Each trustee has an opportunity to serve on the policy committee. He notes:

> I think basically my experience with our policy committee has been that it is very thorough. I'll give you an example. Right now there is a large issue regarding how campuses will treat smoking on campus. The board did a thorough study. They sent questionnaires to

the faculty and the students that asked, "Do you want smoking on campus?" Once the results come back to the policy committee, the committee will bring the results to the full board [for a policy decision]. We are very comfortable and have been, truthfully, rather successful in doing it this way.

One trustee notes that "all of our policies, everything, are dictated by the mission of our college, and anything we do should reflect that mission. That is basically it."

In developing the board agenda, trustees depend upon the president and the president's staff to provide agenda items and to do the work of preparing the agenda. But as one trustee observes, "Any board member can suggest to the chair of our board something that he feels should be discussed on the agenda. The board chair meets with the president to establish the agenda and go over the materials that have been passed out to everybody. We receive a binder of all board materials approximately five days prior to the board meeting." Another board member also states that "any board member who has something he or she would like to have included on the agenda would request it be included; I can't imagine that it would ever be turned down."

One trustee notes that his board has a retreat every year at which the trustees set the board's goals for the year. "Then we have various meetings and establish the benchmark. And we do that throughout the year."

Another trustee notes that her board is in the process of implementing the "policy governance" model of board leadership. She explains:

We are presently attempting to follow the "policy governance" model. I've been on the board for 10 years and I have seen changes, quite drastic changes, but to me embracing change is a lot better than trying to flee from it. The way the board is operating now is with a consent agenda, and we are taking a great deal more time focusing on what we call a visionary agenda and talking about how our college can be better prepared for the future; not knowing exactly what that future might be. We devote a lot of time in our meetings to visioning. So we are spending a lot less time on redundant matters and focusing more on the future.

While not mentioning "policy governance" specifically, one trustee remarks, "The board moves as a corporate body, not as individuals. When we make a decision at the board level, it is a corporate decision. So as a board, when you are functioning and discussing, you let everybody have his or her say. I think that when you set policy, you've got to make sure that the board did it."

Another trustee notes that "we have divided our board into teams based on focus areas. Planning is an ongoing process; I'm proud because we did not do it once and set it aside. In terms of raising issues and being sure that we are staying on course, most issues either originated at the team level or are referred to the team by the board as a whole. I'd like to add [that] the other thing I think we do to make sure that we are doing the right things is that all policies have an expiration date built into them so they have to come back up for review."

Doing the College's Work. John Carver, a leading authority on governing boards, states that the board does not do the community college's work but it must assure that the work is done (Carver & Mayhew, 1994). The trustees interviewed were asked if they agreed with Carver's statement and, if so, how they as trustees assure that the college's work is done. The following responses are some of the answers trustees provided to this question.

One trustee notes that "our board basically deals with policy and with overall governance, and we then pretty much allow the president to develop his plans on how [policies and governance] are to be accomplished. The president usually brings his plans to the board as an agenda item and uses the board as a sounding board. From that point, the president is the one who implements the board policy and the goals of the college."

Another trustee makes his point in a few brief remarks: "Well, the board sets the policy. The administration carries it out. Then you have periodic reports—standards should be established—and you have a procedure to assure that the work is being done by those who report back to the board." Another trustee notes that her board assures that the college's work is done by "surrounding yourself with capable, competent employees. You require that reports be made to the board." Similarly, another trustee notes that his board assures that the work is done through "the delegation of authority, and you pick the best employees you can find. You pay them well. You give them the responsibility and you give them the authority to do the things the board wants done."

Another trustee agrees that the board does not do the work. Indeed, he notes, "I am a kind of person who likes to get involved and a hands-on type person, but once I got elected [to the community college's governing board]

I had to learn that you don't do that in the community college setting. I think a way to check and see that things are followed through on is through personal observations." From another trustee comes the following perspective: "I do agree with the statement. I think that if you do the work, you are getting into micromanagement and that is not what we are there for." From another trustee comes a similar statement: "I agree with the statement. As a board we assure that the work is done through policies that we set and by allowing the staff, the administration, and the faculty to do their work within the range of the policies."

Another trustee feels that "trustees must be informed and knowledgeable about the operations of the college. Is the college going to meet the mission and goals? Trustees must be knowledgeable and informed but not administer." Another trustee feels that the only way to know if the "work is being done" is to have measurable objectives against which to measure board policies. After setting its goals, one trustee's board has the president present the accomplishments of the college to the board. The accomplishments are measured against the board's goals. He notes: "The constant reviewing of the process of goal-making, goal-achieving, and goal-setting helps a board to determine whether or not it is being successful in its mission."

Two trustees note that their governing boards are using "policy governance" to evaluate how well the college's work is being accomplished. One comments:

> I agree with the statement, and as you are probably aware, we have been working for quite a while with the "policy governance" model.

Our whole thrust has been to get away from monitoring the day-to-day operations of the institution. In order to not completely lose sight of these [day-to-day operations], you need to monitor, on some basis, the ends or outcomes as to what's going on. We set goals for the college, for ourselves, and for the administrators, and we are putting in place some standards and ways to check whether those goals are being met. You've got to do that under the "policy governance" model. I think the real danger is if you get too far away from them [day-to-day operations] and don't close the loop and make sure that what they say they are doing is actually getting done. But you do that by setting up and reviewing from time-to-time the overall ends and ask are the goals being met.

A second trustee offers the following observations: "Currently, the greatest challenge is working with our board to understand the 'policy governance' model. It's clear from some of our board's discussions that a number of board members prefer the role of reacting to and approving administrative actions. They are comfortable in the role of 'super managers' and perceive the board position as providing them with status within the community. My long-range goal is to move the board toward a 'policy governance' method of operating."

Another trustee expresses similar thoughts: "I do agree with the statement. What we have tried to do on our board over the last year is to gear our long-range plans to specific areas of concern to the board and develop a reporting mechanism from the institution's employees to tell us what they are doing and how they are doing it in relation to the long-range plans. Nearly every month we get an update on some area that was prioritized in the plans. I think this is how we get the information we need about how we are doing."

Those trustees interviewed appear well aware of the distinction between making policy and "doing the college's work." The dominant theme emerging from the interviews is that after the board makes policies, some means of monitoring the policies must be in place. None of the trustees interviewed appear to want to become overly involved in the day-to-day operations of the college.

Summary
This chapter dealt with some of the activities and commitments trustees can expect to encounter once they accept a position on the governing board. Certainly they will be expected to know something about the wide array of activities in which the college engages. Although the time required of board members is not unreasonable, neither is service on the board to be undertaken without considering that the average trustee spends approximately five hours a week on college business, a substantial amount to spend on volunteer work. On the other hand, the time spent on college activities appears to be relatively free of stress. Most trustees pull their share of the workload and expect the chair to provide leadership for the board.

The interaction among trustees is, for the most part, cordial and cooperative. Most trustees prepare for and attend most board meetings. Trustees realize that although they are responsible for governing the college, many are sensitive about having direct contact with faculty if the contact goes beyond the ceremonial and the social.

Trustees realize that dismissing a president is a serious undertaking with many ramifications. Finally, trustees clearly see their boards as delegating the responsibility of the daily operations of the college to the president and staff. Once the responsibility is delegated, the trustees must monitor the activities of the president and staff to assure that the boards' policies are implemented and their goals achieved.

Trustees

and

the

Community

Community colleges are often called the people's college, democracy's college, or, as their name makes clear, the community's college. The meaning attached to these names depends upon one's perspective and is, therefore, subject to many interpretations.

There is, however, one thing on which most people interested in the community college agree: the mission of the community college is to serve the needs of the people who live in the college's service area.

Working for the People

Trustees are responsible for seeing that the college is responsive to its community and that, as far as possible, the educational needs of the people are met. Carver and Mayhew (1994) note in their book on governing the community college that trustees have a legal and moral responsibility to represent the owners of the college, the people. So if community college boards exist to own the college on behalf of the people, as Carver and Mayhew argue, it follows that a primary concern of trustees is to see that the college's mission is designed to serve its owners, the people. As Carver and Mayhew note, "The board provides the only legitimate bridge between those who morally own the college . . . and the operating organization [the community college]" (p. 25).

Perceptions on Responsiveness. Trustees were asked on the survey how they would rate their responsiveness to certain segments of the community with which most community colleges work. One of the questions was how responsive their governing board is to local and state political leaders. Almost 70% of the trustees believe that their board is very responsive to these leaders; over 28% rate their boards as somewhat responsive; and 2% believe that their board is not very responsive to local and state political leaders (CTS). Because community colleges depend upon state and local political leaders for funding, it is little wonder that over 98% of the trustees rate their board as responsive to these important groups.

Another relationship, and one that community college trustees and presidents have worked very hard to enhance over the last decade or so, is the community college's all-important ties with business and industry. The trustees' responses confirm the importance they attach to the college-business relationship. Over 72% of the trustees rate their board as being very responsive to business leaders, and over 26% rate their board as being somewhat responsive to business leaders (CTS). The trustees' rating of the importance of responding to business leaders is compatible with the emphasis community colleges place on working with business and industry.

Trustees were also asked to rate their board's responsiveness to social agencies. Almost 46% of the trustees rate their board as being very responsive to social agencies; another 48% rate the board as being somewhat responsive; and over 6% believe their board is not very responsive to the leaders of social agencies.

The presidents' survey asked the presidents to rate the responsiveness of their boards in the same three areas rated by the trustees. The ratings by the presidents are quite similar to those of trustees. The presidents rate their boards' responsiveness to political leaders as follows: over 66% rate their board as very responsive, and over 29% rate the board as somewhat responsive. Over 72% of the presidents rate their boards as being very responsive to business leaders, and over 23% rate their board as somewhat responsive. Presidents rate their boards' responsiveness to social leaders as follows: over 38% rate their board as very responsive; almost 54% rate their board as somewhat responsive; and almost 8% rate their board as not very responsive (PS).

That over 72% of the trustees and presidents rated their board as very responsive to business leaders and that 46% of the trustees and 38% of the presidents rated their board as very responsive to social agencies might reflect how trustees and community college presidents view the college's mission and priorities: working with business and industry in economic development, including preparing community college students to compete for highly-skilled jobs, is seen as a higher priority than working with social agencies to solve social problems.

Representing the People. The trustees interviewed were asked for whom they work and whom they represent. Their answers show clearly that trustees hold the college in trust for the public. The trustees interviewed stated, without exception (although the words varied), that they work for the people and are responsible to the people for any and all actions taken by the college on behalf of its constituents. "We represent the people in the district. We also represent the students who come to the college" is one trustee's view. Another states that the "board works for the public. Trustees are the liaison between the public and the college." One trustee feels that she works for the people of the entire state as well as those in the college's service area. Another trustee summarizes his views on the subject: "A trustee's first dedication is to the mission of the college, to its students, and to the community at large. We work directly for the community."

While noting that she, in a sense, works for the governor because he appointed her a trustee, one trustee believes that ultimately all trustees work for and report to the people of the state and the college's service area. "The board works for the community, for the voters. The people we serve are the people in our classes, and they are students of all ages from all walks of life with all kinds of needs. That is what I try to keep foremost in my mind when I am making decisions." Another trustee believes that his board "represents the community, which encompasses a vast diverse background. We also try to represent the group that we are serving, and they are the people who pass through our gates day in and day out."

Based upon the information gathered in the interviews, it is clear that trustees know, without a doubt, that they represent the people who own the college. Board membership is a public trust held on behalf of the people; it is this trust that provides the college with its ethical foundation and from which its mission of serving all segments of the community emanates.

The Community College's Mission

A major function of the community college's governing board is to establish the college's mission. The mission usually is manifested in the form of a mission statement that is widely distributed in the college's catalog, the governing board's manual, self-studies for accreditation, and various other publications. Mission statements represent the most important policy the boards make, and they are revised only after careful consideration by the board and members of the college community. For example, imagine the consequences of a community college board's decision that its institution would no longer be an open access institution but would admit only the top 20% of the high school graduates in its service area. This situation would represent a drastic change in the college's mission and would mean that the college would meet the educational needs of a select few rather than responding to the much broader needs of its service area. Trustees should always keep in mind that the college's mission is the fountain from which all else flows, including all educational programs and services provided by the college.

Understanding the Mission. Chapter 1 of this book discusses the importance of community college trustees understanding and supporting the community college's historic mission. The trustees' survey asked how well board members understand the mission of the community college. Almost 36% perceive trustees to have a thorough understanding of the mission; 43% perceive the understanding to be solid; over 19% believe the understanding to be basic; and 2% feel that trustees have little or no understanding of the community college's mission (CTS).

Presidents were also asked how well board members understand the community college mission. Over 45% of the presidents perceive the understanding to be thorough; over 33% believe it to be solid; almost 20% perceive the understanding to be basic; and over 1% perceive board members to have little or no understanding of the mission (PS).

The majority of the board members are perceived by both trustees and presidents to have a thorough or solid understanding of the mission. On the other hand, the fact that over 21% of the trustees (one out of every five trustees) are perceived to have either a basic or minimal understanding of the mission might be of concern to community college leaders, especially when one looks at how frequently the board considers the mission in making decisions.

The Mission and Decision Making. Trustees were asked how often the board considers the mission of the community college as a basis for decision making. Over 34% state that their board always considers the mission when making decisions; almost 51% state that their board considers the mission most of the time; 13% consider it some of the time; and 1.6% state that the board never considers the mission as a basis for making decisions (CTS).

The perceptions of presidents are similar to those of trustees: 28% of the presidents perceive that the governing board considers the mission as a basis for decision making all of the time; 57% feel that the mission is considered most of the time; almost 14% perceive that it is considered sometimes; and 1.3% of the presidents feel that the governing board never considers the mission as a basis for making decision (PS).

The community college mission is important territory, for the mission defines the college at a given point in time and at a specific location. The majority of the trustees seem well aware of the importance of the college's mission.

Revising the Mission. Trustees were asked on the survey if the college mission had been revised during their term on the board. Over 600 trustees responded to the question.

Almost 18% of the trustees stated that the mission had never been revised during their tenure on the board (74% of these trustees had served on the board four years or less); 40% noted that the mission had been revised once during their tenure. Almost 26% stated that the mission had been revised twice during their tenure, and almost 17% stated that the mission had been revised three or more times during their tenure (CTS).

To put the question into perspective in terms of tenure on the board, recall that the average tenure for all trustees is nearly 8.7 years, and that 51% have served for six years or more (CTS).

With 82% of the trustees revising their college's mission one or more times during their tenure, it is obvious that the mission is not placed on the shelf (a common misconception), to be brought out only when the accrediting team shows up on campus. Moreover, the fact that 18% of the trustees stated they had not revised the mission during their tenure on the board does not necessarily mean that the mission was not at the center of their board's policy debates. One trustee, when asked in an interview if his college considers the college mission when discussing a new program, responded, "Absolutely 100%. At our community college when a new program is being designed or thought about being implemented, the first thing we look at is the mission."

Interpreting Community Needs. The trustees interviewed were asked how their board assures that their college's mission reflects the community needs. One trustee interviewed noted that her college regularly conducts an environmental scan of the college's service area "to anticipate the needs and desires of the community, and then we try to respond to those needs and desires." Another trustee noted that his college employed a consulting firm to determine how the college was perceived by its constituents. "Over 500 individuals were interviewed," he asserted. Another trustee said that his college relies heavily upon curriculum advisory committees to make sure that the college is responding to community needs. "For example, we have a dental hygiene program, and we bring in dental hygienists from around the community to meet with us on a regular basis to make sure we are continuing to teach the latest technology. We do that with every program and attempt to make sure that our programming is relevant to community needs."

Another trustee cautioned that if the college is to be responsive to the community, the college leaders must determine community needs through surveys and other means but must not "sit back and wait for the community to be involved with the college." Another trustee said, "We are pretty active. Our board is pretty active with the community and we get input; we have open meetings for the budget. We have different forums on our different campuses. Students all have very strong organizations and they are part of our meetings. The union sits at the table at every board meeting. So we have pretty open communications."

One trustee recommends that there be constant communications between the trustees and the community. One approach he suggests is trustee appearances at service clubs. He also notes that he works closely with the seven public school districts in the college's service area. "Three times a year we invite them to dinner at the college, and we discuss items of common interest." The guest list includes 35 school board members, as well as the superintendents of the seven school districts.

One trustee noted that, in addition to its curriculum advisory committees, her college uses focus groups made up of community members as a means of obtaining information and advice from the community.

> At the board level, we asked for nominations to serve on focus groups in each of the 15-county areas we serve. In each county, there is at least one focus group from secondary education, from industry, from parents, and from students. We kind of identified constituencies and sent out board invitations, and we [trustees] led discussions about what we are doing, what we should be doing that we are not doing, and what could we be doing better. And the board will repeat this activity, not every year, but I think at a minimum every three years.

As suggested in chapter 1, community college trustees are constantly on the firing line in the sense that they daily "bump into the community." This bumping often works to some trustees' advantage. One trustee notes, for example, that "we get input from the community by listening and talking. I'm from a rural area so that makes it different from being in a city environment. By listening and just by visiting with the people at different functions and different activities where our conversations overlap, I find out what the people are thinking. If I have a specific need, I will try to contact other people in the area."

One trustee whose college surveyed the community to test the college's name recognition was pleasantly pleased to report that over 80% of the people in the college's service area knew about the college. Another trustee states that "anytime I have the opportunity to get before a civic group, I will take the opportunity, not only to communicate what is going on at the college but to solicit feedback from the community."

Closing the Loop. Trustees work for the people; they solicit information from the people for whom they work. Therefore, it seems logical that if a public servant solicits advice from the public, the public should have some indication of what happens once the advice is given. The most common methods of providing information to the community are through annual reports, news releases, press conferences, announcements of course offerings, research reports, graduation and other public ceremonies, curriculum advisory committee meetings, media representatives' attendance at public board meetings, and regularly scheduled meetings with community groups.

Proceeding on the assumption that trustees provide feedback to community members, the trustees interviewed were asked how they close the loop between information solicited from the public and sharing with the public how the information is used.

One good example of closing the loop comes from the college that uses focus groups to obtain information from the community. The trustee quoted above notes, "You know, all of those who participated in the focus groups got the college's long-range plan since they were involved very early in the planning. We said, 'Here is what we have today that you contributed to, and we would like to invite you to send comments. What do we need to do next?' So we try to create an ongoing loop."

Another trustee notes that, while his board does not actually relay the results of community surveys to community members, "we take the information and work with it in getting more of our programs out to the public to make people more aware of what we have; and, we use the information [gathered from the public] to develop new programs." One trustee, when asked if the college would develop new courses and programs based upon input from the community, responded, "Absolutely! We would have the specific courses or events that the community would be looking for."

Any number of the trustees interviewed noted that the public was kept informed through the avenues mentioned earlier such as press releases, mailing of class schedules, public service ads, and other avenues one normally associates with the public information office of a community college. Several trustees felt the personal touch was important in keeping the public informed. One trustee notes that it is important for her college to work closely with the business community, four-year institutions, and the public schools. She wants the public to know how successful the college is in placing students in jobs and how successful students are who transfer to four-year colleges and universities. These measures, she feels, are important to the college and to the community. "I think the transfer rates and having some kind of placement tracking through business is one way of measuring [how we meet community needs]." In addition, she notes that the college has a very active board and this results in "conversations with people in all kinds of venues. I think, just in general, when you move about the community and identify yourself or are known as being involved with the college as a trustee, people will just start speaking to you about the college. And you can encourage that, of course."

One trustee offers an excellent summary with which to conclude this discussion on closing the loop between community input and letting the community know what impact its input has had on the college. She comments as follows:

> The only way I have been able to figure out that we can do it [keep the public informed] is for the board to have goals that are measurable and to say this is what we want to have happen and put it in terms so we can determine whether or not it has happened. It is easy to say we want to be fiscally responsible, and we don't want to be in debt and that kind of thing. But when we get into programs, I don't think it is enough to say we want a good program. We have to say what kind of program we want in terms of output. We want a program whereby our students can transfer to four-year institutions; we want a program that gives our students the competencies that employers in our communities demand. I get lots of phone calls and lots of letters. I answer all of the letters and phone calls myself. We get very good coverage in the newspaper. If we feel like we haven't gotten good coverage, I write letters to the editor to try to communicate something that I think has not been reported back to the community in an appropriate way. We have had press conferences the board called when we felt like it was something very important that we wanted the community to know.

The trustees interviewed recognize the importance of obtaining the views of community members and of sharing with the community the actions that their views help shape. In one way or another, each trustee noted the importance of trustees being active in the community and of maintaining personal contact with those individuals whom the college was created to serve.

Representation on the Board

As was pointed out in chapter 2, the percentages of trustees who are Caucasian and male do not reflect the makeup of many communities served by community colleges. The composition of the governing boards raise some interesting and important questions.

Should the governing boards of the people's college reflect more accurately the membership of the communities the colleges serve? Or does it matter as long as the total population is adequately represented by the college's governing board? If it were determined to be desirable to have governing boards that are more reflective of community membership, is it practical or even possible to achieve this composition? Questions regarding board composition seemed to be important enough to ask both trustees and presidents in the interviews if boards of trustees should reflect more accurately the composition of the community. Prior to asking the question, those interviewed were given the current percentages of trustees who are Caucasian and male. The following responses to the question illustrate its complexity.

Trustees. "I think the answer is an adamant 'yes'. The only excuse for having board members who do not reflect the overall demographics is when there has been a search and no one has been found. But I think it should be a top priority" is one trustee's answer to the question. From another trustee comes the following analysis: "I would think that it [representation on the board reflecting the community] brings a perspective that can be easily missed. In this state we have a very high percentage of Hispanics. There is a culture you miss if you don't have someone with you who is a part of it."

Another trustee has the following perspective: "I feel every effort should be made to have a board composed of a cross section of the community—male, female, race. But in reality sometimes people are not willing to seek out those positions, so you can't force someone to apply for a position if they do not have the interest." From another trustee comes this statement: "Boards should and must be [representative] if they are going to draw students into their educational system. But I feel very strongly—I am Hispanic—I feel very strongly that the board should reflect the people served in the community colleges."

One trustee leaves little doubt where he stands on the subject of board composition reflecting student-community diversity.

> Well, first, that is an absolute. I mean we are living in 1996. If you have taxpayers and our community colleges operate on tax dollars, those tax dollars are from the entire population within the county which is made up of various ethnic groups. They should be represented. There is not much more I need to say on that. I think if we don't wake up to that and really put it in place now, we're going to lose. We are looking at the year 2000. No longer do we need to be looking back at the way things have been run in the 80s, 70s, and 60s.

Another trustee gave the following response to the question on board composition:

> Ideally, I think the board should reflect the demographic makeup of the community. In practice, it is not so easy. In Florida a couple

of years ago a law was proposed that would have required the governor to adhere to some very strict guidelines as far as ethnic groups and gender are concerned in making board appointments. I think if you get into some very specific rules or requirements like this, you run the risk of not getting the best person for the job. There is some irony in this question, for our board was and is mostly female. Our board would have had to have been changed for artificial reasons. But do I think it is desirable? I think it is desirable to have [diverse representation on the board] because if we don't know other cultures very well we may be insensitive to things. If the various cultures are represented, this sensitivity is likely to be heightened.

Another trustee responded as follows: "This is a tough one because on the one hand I really do believe that the people who comprise the population of the college should have a voice in making some of those [board] decisions." She continues, "What you do want regardless of ethnicity or gender are people with influence in the community or knowledge of the community and a commitment to the college. One would hope that those people can be drawn from various ethnic groups. But just tokenism where you fill up the board with the same percentage of ethnicity that you have in the community in and of itself is not particularly useful." From another, "Yes, I feel the board should reflect the makeup of the communities. If not in direct proportions, it should be working toward that goal of reflecting more the demographics of the community. I know it is not always an easy situation, but I feel the board should be made aware of it and should be working towards that goal."

The trustees interviewed obviously realize the importance of having various segments of the community represented on the board.

Presidents. Community college presidents and those who want to be presidents have an interest in the composition of the governing board for a number of reasons. First, to restate the obvious, trustees select presidents and presidents work for governing boards. The composition of the board *may* influence that selection and, perhaps, the relations between the board and president. For example, in 1991, 89% of the community college presidents were white and 89% were men (Vaughan, Mellander, & Blois, 1994). Although the percentage of female presidents has increased since 1991, the perception might be that governing boards select presidents who, up to a point, reflect the makeup of the governing board. Second, presidents have the primary responsibility for seeing that the college mission developed and approved by the board is achieved. In carrying out the community college's mission of serving all segments of the community, presidents need inroads into all segments, inroads that can be provided by trustees. Third, presidents need to understand the perspectives of current and future students. If the president is a white male, his perspective might be broadened by having a board with both female and minority representation. How, then, do presidents view having a board with racial and gender balance?

As was true with the trustees, presidents were given the percentage of minorities and women that make up community college boards nationally prior to being asked if their boards should reflect more accurately the makeup of their communities. The following are their responses.

One president notes, "As you develop relationships with your board, the relationship carries over to the relationships you have outside the college. With a good balanced board, you are able to develop relationships with the different elements of the community. I think the board should reflect the makeup, then whatever element is out there always has an avenue to give input into the college, and they don't feel cut off and isolated by the college."

Another president, while endorsing balance on the board, suggests that there are other considerations that are equally important:

> That's a good question. It's always desirable to have the board reflect the general conditions of the community. If you are in a town that has a more proportionate minority community, it would be important to have minority members on the board so they can help translate those special interpretations of what the college could do and does do for its community. I find, however, that fairness, equity, careful and cautious deliberation, and statesmanship, intelligence, and sensitivity, are all equally distributed in the population. I find that having one particular representation on the board does not solve any other shortcomings should they be found on the board. In some cases, minority leadership doesn't guarantee that you are going to have solutions in the community.

From a president of a large urban institution with an elected board come the following observations:

> I think it's important that a board that is holding the college in trust for the community in some way reflects the interests of the community. I do not think that it necessarily follows that to reflect

the interests, one must be of those interests. In other words, you don't have to divide up the community and say, okay, you have 70% Hispanics in your community and you want 70% Hispanics on your board. I don't think representative democracy requires that. It does not require anything other than that you represent the community, and I do not think that it necessarily means that you must be one-to-one in representation. Having said that, we must also recognize that those persons are elected whom the community wants to represent it. We have to accept that and not try to orchestrate it to fit a particular recipe that we think is critical. I'm not saying that it is not important to have appropriate representation, but that must be left with the electorate. It must make those determinations.

Another president, who has experienced his share of controversy recently, takes a pragmatic view of trying to have a board with representation that reflects the makeup of the college and community. His views are extensive and are reproduced, almost in full, below.

I think we should have balance on the board so we are aware of concerns of the constituents in the community. But that leads to a terrible situation where every person in a community, every group in the community, feels he or she should be represented. For instance, I can speak with experience; here at [my] community college we have some persons in the community who have a very, very conservative view. We think they represent a minority, but they are demanding that their views be represented on the board. Now their view is a very narrow view, and it's a view that really deals with only one aspect of the curriculum, a very significant aspect of the curriculum, but it would trouble me if they were allowed to have a seat on the board simply because, as one legislator told me, they should be heard also. There are vehicles for people in the community to be heard, and those vehicles are to have open meetings of your board and to allow all members of the community to have access to the board. We do that by allowing any member of the community to speak for three minutes on any agenda item, and at the end of the board meeting to speak about anything they want to speak about with respect to the college. So I think that's a way to give community access, but I think you have to be careful not to begin to develop quotas. In our case, there are people who appoint board members, so we must encourage the people in positions of power who make those appointments to be sensitive to the needs of the community. By the same token, I think we have to avoid the concept of a quota because that can really lead to a lot of divisiveness when people begin to count noses, and it becomes almost impossible to satisfy in a 10-person board the broad spectrum of different views in a community. I've always advocated that we have the very best board members, and I hope that when those board members come, they represent the diversity we are looking for. But I think you have to approach it from that vantage point first before we say let's approach it from a diversity standpoint and then hope that they come with good credentials.

Quotes from several other presidents serve to summarize how presidents view board representation. Each paragraph represents the views of a different president.

I think we should have representation that reflects the community makeup. Here we have a large Hispanic community. [In one county] we have a large number of Hispanics who have lived in that community for 80 years and have never had a school board member or a community college trustee. They have never had a city council person to represent them, and I believe very strongly that they need to have representation on the college board because of a large number of people who should be attending the college but are not. Every time an opening comes up, I start talking to the board chair about looking at getting a Hispanic person. We came close. We had a resignation and had the opportunity to interview and select a board member between now and the next election. We had a person all lined up to interview and she, in the end, decided not to be interviewed.

I think it is one of those things that if you don't work it out, you do end up with pretty much an all-white, male board. If a substantial part of your community is not represented on the board, then you have to make extraordinary efforts in other areas to offset that.

I think it's great that the board would be more reflective of the community, but I guess you'd have to ask the question in what ways, because there are many facets of communities. Communities are extremely complex, much more complex than their ethnicity or gender. I think board members who are strong members have a strong sense of community and are able to understand the various facets of the community and make decisions accordingly.

Absolutely boards should reflect the makeup, and the reason is because . . . we are the community's college. The only way we can be the community's college is to be connected with the various constituents of our various communities.

I view the board as representative of the ownership of the institution, and if there is no connection with the ownership or if there is no ethnic representation, it is very hard for a board to represent that ownership.

I think it's important whenever possible that trustees reflect the community at large. In situations where they are elected, that's not always easy to pull off. But I think the institution is better served by having people who can speak for the various constituent groups.

Can or should trustees influence the composition of their governing boards? Perhaps. But should presidents? Most presidents take a "hands off" approach to board membership, especially if the board is elected. Nevertheless, based upon the first author's experience, presidents often surreptitiously (some presidents are quite open about their choices) influence the selection for board membership. Indeed, 12% of the trustees, when asked how they became involved with their community college board, stated that their involvement was encouraged by the college president (CTS).

Although it is beyond the scope of this discussion to answer the above questions about board selection in detail, some generalizations can be drawn. The trustees interviewed perceive balanced minority representation to be an important consideration for community college governing boards. (There was very little discussion on gender.) Presidents are more cautious about recommending that the balance be present. Can boards change the current situation? Trustees can work with other board members and community leaders to identify a pool of potential minority and female trustees and encourage them to seek election or appointment to the board, assuming these groups are not adequately represented and are not aggressively seeking representation on the board. Those boards that are permitted to fill unexpired terms on the board can select minorities or women to fill vacancies, assuming these groups are under-represented on the board. In any event, whether boards can or should achieve a balance in terms of female or minority representation, all trustees have the right and responsibility to represent all segments of the communities served by their college. This goal can never be compromised, regardless of the board's composition.

Summary

Nothing is more important to trustees than assuring that the public trust granted them manifests itself through service to the community. When viewed through the eyes of trustees, the term "the people's college" takes on new meaning. Not only does the term signify that the college responds to the community but also that the college belongs to the people. Holding the college in trust is seen as an important responsibility for trustees. The avenue through which the college responds to the community—to the people—is through its mission, a mission that is analyzed, debated, endorsed, and (when needed) revised by the governing board. Trustees realize that if their community college is to serve community needs, the governing board and college administration must know what those needs are. A number of ways are used to determine community needs. As public servants, trustees feel a responsibility to inform community members of what actions the board has taken as a result of discussions with community members. The number of minorities and women serving on community college governing boards raises some questions that trustees and presidents must struggle with as the nation's population becomes more diverse.

Satisfaction from Serving

Chapter 1 of this book raised the question, "Why would anyone want to serve as a community college trustee?" A number of answers to this question are provided in chapter 1 and subsequent chapters.

It seemed, however, that the best way to answer the question was to ask the trustees how they felt about service on their governing board. With this thought in mind, trustees were asked in the survey what they found most rewarding about serving as a community college trustee. Although the question required a narrative answer rather than a multiple choice response, almost 600 trustees responded to the question. While some answers were fairly brief, others were over a typed page in length. Their comments, with a few exceptions, are quite positive.

These responses provide insights into why community college trustees choose to serve on their governing boards and describe some of the satisfactions they derive from serving. In order to preserve the flavor as well as the content of their observations, trustees tell the story of their service in their own words. The comments are organized under the headings of serving the community, serving the college, serving the student, and personal satisfactions from serving. Few of the observations fall into these neat categories; rather, in many cases, there is some overlapping among categories. Nevertheless, the groupings help focus the trustees' observations. It is hoped the groupings will assist the reader in following the thread that weaves from community, to college, to student, to governing board, to individual, as trustees sort out the joys (and in some few cases the frustrations) of serving on the governing boards of their community colleges.

Serving the Community

A large number of trustees asserted that serving their community is the most satisfying aspect of being a member of their community college's board of trustees. When asked on the survey to give their reasons for becoming involved with the community college's governing board, 14% of the trustees stated that they became involved because they had been a student at a community college and now wanted to give something back to the community by serving on the board (CTS). For example, one trustee wants to "return to the community the gifts I've been granted through higher education."

A board chair feels that "the most rewarding aspects of chairing a community college governing board are those of being able to have input and influence in causing the community college to serve almost any interested citizen and to contribute to the economic development of the district. Knowing that the community college provides educational programs for a wide variety of community needs gives one (at least me) a great deal of satisfaction from being involved in such an adventure!" Another trustee enjoys "being a community opinion shaper," and another enjoys the "sense of returning something to the community." "We need education if any semblance of democracy is to be preserved" is the way one trustee expresses satisfaction.

Another trustee says, "Knowledge that the community college can serve so many members of the community's population." Another enjoys "helping provide an excellent education to people in our community at a reasonable cost and making it accessible." Another trustee expresses satisfaction and gratitude from "putting back into society the help that I received and being able to participate in the growth and development of a fine community college with a focus of excellence. The involvement also helped me in my own personal development." "Playing a positive leadership role in the community and seeing the numerous and varied ways in which the college enhances the community" is rewarding for one trustee. "Being able to observe the positive impact the college has on the community" offers rewards for another trustee. "I enjoy participating in community affairs in general and consider such participation a necessary part of citizenship. The community college fills in gaps for all types of people," notes another trustee.

These statements are additional trustees' comments from the survey. Each statement is from a different trustee.

The opportunity to make contributions toward improving the quality of life in the community.

The chance to use my varied background as an adult educator, manager, and union steward to have an impact on our community college.

The opportunity to bring business needs to the college and let the business community learn what the college has to offer.

Being a positive force in my community; giving something back; helping people improve their lifestyles.

The opportunity to make a contribution to the success of an asset in our local community.

Our small (24,000 people) community owes much of the credit for the vitality of our businesses and schools to the community college. I feel proud to serve on the board and to contribute in a small way to my town.

A feeling of contributing to the success of the community in which I live (not just the success of the president and board).

The rewards, when they occur, far offset the frustrations. Helping to build our society, both collectively and individually; improving the quality of life and economic impact provided by educating our people; the satisfaction of being a part of an effort to uplift and reach into the future by reaching a vision; knowing that this is a way to make the world better.

Serving my community and contributing to the future of our community. I view the college as one of the most important institutions in our community and am proud to serve on its board.

To continue serving the needs of the community and to assist in the advancement of this service is a rewarding commitment.

Since there is no monetary reward as a trustee, my satisfaction is in knowing I have listened to the public's desires for education in the community college and in fulfilling that request.

My community supports me. Trusteeship gives me an opportunity to support my community.

Sense of serving the public; feeling of making the community a better place; opportunity to use my experience for the community's good.

I derive great satisfaction from working with an institution that is at the very hub of economic and employment activity and from working continuously to define and refine the institution's mission and roles so as to most effectively meet the diverse needs of our constituents. In short, what I am doing contributes a lot of good to the community around me.

The responsibility to help provide citizens with opportunities to improve and enhance their lives through education is very rewarding to me as a community college trustee.

Being involved and part of an institution that is working toward higher education and learning for all people in the community is important. It's a good feeling to see community leaders giving back to their community and sharing their experiences by working together for a common goal: higher education for all which provides a better community to live in.

The demands on a good trustee require skills that I took a lifetime to develop. I enjoy using them in serving my community.

The desire to serve one's community is high on the list of satisfactions enjoyed by trustees. Community college board membership does indeed provide trustees with an avenue for "giving back to the community." Service to the community is the goal of many trustees; the means for accomplishing this is through serving on the community college board of trustees.

Serving the College

Trustees serve their colleges in many ways. Their comments on serving the college demonstrate that they have the institution's overall welfare at heart, whether service consists of setting the mission, policy formulation, or working to create a more effective governing board. In almost every case, those trustees commenting on serving the college share a sense of pride and joy in the accomplishments of the college. The following observations give the reader a sense of just how deeply some trustees feel about service on the board.

One trustee feels "blessed with the opportunity to serve on a board. Our shared governance and collaborative problem-solving mechanism are bringing together all parts of the college: classified staff, faculty, administration, and board." Another trustee likes "having the board discuss matters and come to a mutually satisfying conclusion as a group. We can come to a common consensus even if we don't all agree, and no one leaves with hard feelings. We all work together so well, and that includes the president and administration."

One can almost feel the excitement one trustee feels about being on the board: "Visioning, process, and application; seeing direction change when the board and president work together; results! It is also great to see faculty and students express their pleasure with the college." Another trustee notes that "being a part of the learning organization, influencing necessary changes that will affect future learners, and working with a talented, professional president and staff" in setting the vision and shaping the mission are important aspects of being on the governing board.

Resolving conflicts that occur among board members is satisfying to one veteran trustee: "Having served almost four full (six-year) terms, I have developed skills in mediating opposing and even conflicting opinions. I think

I contribute a 'middle way' that keeps things moving, yet skirts creating division." Another trustee finds satisfaction in "the opportunity to promote and advocate for 'pay check education' and promote and encourage literacy training."

"To know I have helped provide the leadership in developing, organizing, and supporting the college in a way so the many students who pass through the doors have a better life," provides one trustee with satisfaction. Another trustee says, "Participating in the development of policy on the curriculum committee, especially as it directly impacts student course development, is very rewarding." Similar observations come from another trustee: "The feeling that I am helping to establish policy and direction for a significant community asset is rewarding." From another: "I have participated in a recent shift of my board from a captive board subservient to the college president to a strong, independent board that is redirecting the college from bureaucracy to student-community service."

As a community college advocate, one trustee enjoys "promoting and communicating the changing mission of the community college in our community; helping start new colleges and getting areas annexed into our district; and helping bring fiscal responsibility into decisions and the planning process." Another trustee gets satisfaction from "providing general and financial management and emphasis to the board for its legal and fiduciary responsibilities." "The ability and opportunity to work with a great staff who are intelligent, innovative, and dedicated to providing quality education to students of all ages in our community" brings another trustee satisfaction. Shaping the college mission is important to others: "As a community college trustee, I have the opportunity to influence what areas of training and what educational programs will be offered in our communities." "The most rewarding aspect of being a community college trustee is setting policy for a college that has an open-door policy."

Two trustees get satisfaction from seeing the board move in new directions. From one: "My board has been receiving training in the 'policy governance' model for the past 13 months. I believe the board will *fully* commit to this model in the near future. This is exciting. The board adopted . . . a resolution I proposed committing the institution to provide quality education and services based on the concepts and principles of Deming, Juran, Scholtes, and the like. These areas of board involvement are truly exciting to me as a trustee." From another comes this statement of satisfaction:

> Working as a team member to advance the interests of the college is very rewarding. There is a very real sense that the board is more than the sum total of the individual views and opinions of the constituent members. Helping the board and administration to realize the value of properly focused policy work is another enjoyable aspect. More than once the board has strayed into the zone of 'administrivia'; when this has been highlighted, the board has fallen back into a more properly defined zone of action. We have made considerable progress in moving the board toward having and pushing its own agenda rather than sitting there like 'potted plants' and enjoying the food and nutrients that the administration brings to it. The notion of 'board empowerment' has resulted in renewed focus on the board's policy agenda for the future and has resulted in many positive changes in the organization's overall health.

One trustee, in addition to learning about new programs and keeping current on education, legislation, and other issues, finds it "rewarding to know policies and procedures and to ensure that everyone from students to administrators is being treated fairly." "The satisfaction of providing leadership, of setting policy, of selecting the president, and assessing accountability in fulfilling the mission" is how one trustee views serving on the board. Another observes, "The most rewarding aspect of being a trustee is implementing changes that will carry through the next 10 to 15 years: changes that will impact on uplifting standards and results for women, returning students, and minorities give me a sense of personal and professional satisfaction." Another trustee enjoys having the "ability to direct the college, through the president, to serve the community, and to provide a fine educational facility for our area."

A number of trustees expressed their pleasure in getting to know and working with the college's faculty and staff. These quotes reflect the feelings of many of the trustees regarding working with members of the college community:

The association with community college people, people who are the most caring group I've known, is my greatest pleasure as a trustee.

The pleasure comes from being a member of a winning team, the prize being the empowerment in people's lives. I can't imagine any public service that could possibly compare with this experience.

The most rewarding thing about chairing a community college governing board is the opportunity to associate with the high quality people on its board, its staff, and faculty.

My friendship with the board, the president, and the administrative staff is very rewarding.

Based upon the above, trustees are committed to leading and directing the college administration through the president to improve the college's outcomes and image. They take great pride in providing this leadership. Although the above responses are limited in the sense that they focus on what trustees enjoy about serving on their governing board rather than upon the hard work and occasional frustrations they encounter, it is nevertheless clear from their remarks that these trustees are thinking and acting at a level commensurate with their roles as board members. For example, the comments on mission, governance, policy, and working as a team member tend to allay the fears that trustees are interested in "micro-managing" the institution.

Serving Students

Those trustees commenting on the rewarding aspects of serving on their college's governing board appear to have their priorities in order as to why the college exists. Although *service to the community* is the governing board's goal and although *the college* is the *means* for achieving that goal, trustees realize that *the product* of it all is student learning. Many of the trustees surveyed commented on the rewards inherent in seeing students improve their lives, noting that for many of these students the community college represents their only hope for a higher education.

The graduation ceremony as a symbol of student success is special for a number of trustees. As one trustee observes, "The graduation ceremony is very rewarding because it focuses on student success stories. This is what

I find most rewarding." The comments from other trustees about graduation convey the ceremony's importance to them as board members.

The other thrills come at ESL [English as a second language] graduation, high school diploma graduation, and regular graduation. They are all quite different celebrations with the common realization that education is going to make a big difference in the lives of those who stuck with the task.

Graduation: to see the varied age groups earn a degree to get a job. The general community respect the college receives makes me very proud!

Signing the degrees and certificates for the graduating students and wishing them a great return on their education is most rewarding.

I attend graduation each year and am renewed.

Attending awards ceremonies and graduation are high points.

To see the faces of young and old alike when they receive recognition at graduation creates a sense of pride and power; it gives you a feeling of being both big and small. I love it.

The most rewarding compensation I receive as a community college trustee is when I attend graduation exercises and see hundreds of graduates reach a goal that will improve the quality of life for them, and I realize this would not have been possible for them if it had not been for our community college.

Graduation. Knowing that we've made higher education available and watching the faces of family and graduates.

Being able to attend graduation and see the pride and gleam of hope for the graduates' future.

Trustees, then, show their pride and satisfaction in the college's core function: providing education for students from all segments of society. For some trustees, seeing students graduate serves as the symbol and culmination of the work of the governing board.

Personal Satisfaction

After leaving the community college presidency following 17 years in the position, the first author of this book was asked what he missed most about the presidency. His answer? "Being president." A number of trustees, when asked what they enjoy most about being a trustee, gave a similar response. Their answer? "Being a trustee." Certainly there is nothing wrong with and much right with individuals enjoying the prestige, recognition, and sense of accomplishment that comes with public service. Serving as a community college trustee is no exception: trustees do enjoy the personal satisfactions that come with service on the board. For example, one board chair expresses great pride and satisfaction from serving. "As you can see, I pop my buttons because of what we do." Another chair is "treated like gold" following each board meeting. These quotes, taken from the survey, further illustrate the satisfaction that comes from serving on the board.

Public service and community involvement have always been an important part of my life and being a trustee has provided a very meaningful retirement. Lucky me!

The first reason [for serving on the board] is a selfish one; it allows me to continue to keep in touch with educators and the world of education.

I am a member of a very important board.

Personal satisfaction in guiding the largest and one of the highest rated community colleges in California.

I love having a platform from which to advocate positive change and improvement of public education.

It is a distinct honor to be appointed by the governor to serve as a community college trustee.

It [service on the governing board] keeps me busy and occupied with things I know how to do and maintains my relationships with other people who have similar backgrounds.

The returns (inclusion in the self-study, roasts-toasts, child care center progress, hugs from faculty) I get from staff, including administrators, who respect my respect for them and the opportunity to get a hug or handshake from a student I may have helped with a problem along the way are my rewards.

I get a certain amount of prestige and a lot of personal satisfaction.

[As chair] I enjoy the prestige, because your opinions have more impact on other board members, administration, and teachers as well as the community.

Being able to attend various state and national meetings to hear what other schools are doing.

My friendship with the board, the president, and his administrative staff is rewarding.

Prestige and acceptance of fellow board members from the community and elected officials.

[As chair] bringing harmony to a board that has undergone some major problems last year.

Trustees obviously find that satisfactions from serving on the board accrue to the individual board members through any number of avenues. Were this not the case, many trustees might be less willing to serve as community college trustees.

Frustrations

Based upon the survey responses, negative comments about serving as a community college trustee were rare; indeed, a total of eight trustees out of the almost 600 who responded to the question regarding satisfactions from serving find service on the governing board to be somewhat frustrating. Their insights bring into perspective a viewpoint that, while expressed by only a small number of trustees, helps one to comprehend the complex and, at times, frustrating aspects of fulfilling the trustee's role.

One board chair's comments, while expressing frustration more than negativism, makes it clear that serving as a community college trustee, and especially as board chair, is both frustrating and stressful at times. "This is a very hard job. We have so many factions within the board and within the college that it is impossible to know how votes on certain issues will go or what will happen at the meeting. It can be very draining. As chair, I have more power and control over the meetings than anyone else. It is rewarding when I can steer the meeting in a direction I think is most appropriate."

Another trustee takes a swipe at other trustees, faculty members, affirmative action and other government regulations and requirements, students, and the community college in general. This trustee also offers advice to the authors of this book.

> I'm amazed our board functions as well as it does. Board members' biases get in the way of the college's best interests. Tenured teachers, lowered academic standards (to keep enrollment up and federal and state money coming in), the multitude of government regulations, excessive requirements for the handicapped, constraints put upon the school due to overzealous compliance with affirmative action, disruptive student and teacher activists (only a few but a lot of noise) are just a few of the reasons we can expect at best mediocre and at least poor educational outcomes. You could probably forget the survey [the one conducted by the authors of this book] and spend the money getting at the above and achieve a lot more!

For two trustees, frustration comes from the bureaucracy associated with the trustee's role at their colleges. One of the trustees observes, "I find it very frustrating to be a trustee at our local community college because I feel like all we do is approve administrative reports, sort of another layer of administration. There's no real governance at this time." The other trustee offers some very positive observations, as well as sharing some frustrations. From the positive side comes this statement:

> Each commencement and honors convocation reminds me that our college is extremely important to the lives of each of our students and, therefore, to the entire community. What we hear is amazing,

heart warming, and energizing, because we can see and hear concrete examples of success over what could be insurmountable obstacles.

From the negative side:

But, when I'm bogged down with bi-monthly meeting notebooks full of minutiae, I want to quit. We're trying to get summaries preceding the pages of information. Once in a while, we get some but not enough. I cannot stand the faculty's petty grievances, self-centeredness, and lack of courage to try new methods; thank God they're in the minority!

Anyone who has ever served on a governing board or as president of a community college understands that the positions have inherent frustrations.

Summary

The story that unfolds in this chapter, more than any of the other chapters in this book, is told in the words of the trustees. As their comments indicate, almost all trustees view their role as rewarding. Serving the community is the goal of most trustees; the college is the avenue through which the service is provided, and student learning and achievement are the products of trustees' efforts. Serving on the governing board of their community college is viewed by the majority of the trustees as an honorable, exciting, worthy, and enjoyable way to pay their civic rent.

Because so much of the above is in the words of trustees, it seems fitting to close this chapter with the perspective of two trustees, both of whom provide commentary that captures the essence of trusteeship for many of those individuals who currently lead the nation's community colleges. Their words follow, with each paragraph representing the perspective of a trustee.

Rewards of serving on the governing board: (1) Representing the people in the community who are paying for the services the college provides, most of whom are honest, hard-working people who never had the chance for an education themselves; being sure their tax dollars are not wasted; (2) Seeing people who are seriously trying to improve their lives and the lives of their families by learning something to make them *productive* citizens in our society; (3) Being associated with a fine institution with truly dedicated and inspired employees who view their jobs as a calling, and who have a heart for their students; (4) Speaking out as an objective observer.

The community college is an exciting intersection of academia and practical affairs. The institution must strive for academic excellence while also providing training programs. My work as a trustee has opened up new ways of thinking about economic, social, and political challenges. In particular, community colleges seem to hold a critical role in the economic future of the middle class. I have learned about how an institution works, how it can change, and what possibilities it can open up for a community.

The Perfect Fit

Trustees have a good idea of what they seek in presidents. To explore this topic further, those trustees who were interviewed were asked what they looked for in a president.

What, they were asked, were those things that produced a good fit—a good match—between the president and the college.

Looking at the other side of the same coin, presidents, while hoping for a match made in heaven when they assume a presidency, discover all too soon that all presidential matches are made in the boardroom and on the college campus, and not in heaven. Therefore, presidents must work effectively with their governing board if they are going to be successful. Those presidents interviewed were also asked what they considered to be a good fit between the governing board and president. In exploring the question, the presidents were asked what their own governing board would look like if they, the presidents, could choose it.

The following presents the views of the trustees and presidents as they envision their "perfect match." Trustees and presidents can learn much from each other's perceptions of what makes an outstanding board and president.

Trustees' Ideal President

What, then, do trustees look for in a president? One theme that emerged from the interviews centered around the president's ability to look beyond the college's day-to-day activities. Some trustees identified this quality as the ability to shape and articulate a vision for the college. Others used the term long-range planning. Others wanted a president who is able to communicate the college's mission in ways that the public understands and therefore supports. All trustees, it can be assumed, want presidents who possess skills, personal attributes, and characteristics that enhance their ability to lead a college.

The Vision. One trustee believes that "community members have to understand where the president wants to take the institution and have to buy into that leadership direction. If they don't, you are looking for trouble in that respect, particularly for our community college. I think it is very important that our president be perceived as someone who is trying to get advanced higher education to our community." Another trustee notes that the president must have a vision with definite goals for achieving that vision. A trustee wants a "person who has vision for the future and who can look forward and use leadership skills to guide the institution in the way that the president and the board have decided it should move." From another: "I look for vision. That is, what is the president's dream about what our institution is doing and should be doing; where is that individual going to take us?" One trustee's comments summarize the need for a president to have vision. She notes, "We want a person who will lead the college into the future."

Presidents too are aware of the importance of vision in a leader. One president notes that "although a president does many things, the two qualities that distinguish highly effective presidents from the others are that the effective president has vision and [that she or he] provides leadership in achieving that vision; the effective board recognizes, values, nurtures, and supports these qualities."

The ideal president, then, should have a good understanding of where the college is going and how it is going to get there. Call it vision, long-range planning, or the ability to interpret and communicate the institutional mission, the ability to move the college toward planned goals is an important characteristic of the president. The vision must have benchmarks—objectives—that can be measured to determine if the college is moving toward achieving its vision. If the vision for the college is to serve all segments of the population adequately, it is difficult to say when or if that vision has been achieved. One can, however, measure the increase in minority enrollments, the number of students enrolling from various segments of the college service area, the number of graduates who successfully transfer and complete the four-year degree, and the number of students employed in their chosen fields upon graduation. The ideal president will combine vision with a plan for achieving that vision. The ideal president will work with the governing board to shape the vision and to develop plans for moving toward achieving it.

Skills and abilities. Not surprisingly, trustees want presidents with certain skills and abilities, for without them the vision is likely to be little more than a hollow promise. Although trustees should be able to assume that presidents have honed their skills and increased their knowledge about leadership prior to assuming the presidency, some things just cannot be taken for granted when seeking the ideal president; certain skills and abilities must be present.

Prominent among the skills and abilities required in the ideal president is the ability to communicate, with special emphasis on communicating the college's mission to the community. One trustee wants "a person who is articulate, a person who is a good communicator." Noting that some community college trustees are elected to serve on the governing board with the support of a special interest group, one trustee believes that the president must have the skills to help the different factions reach consensus.

From another trustee comes this perspective: "I think we need someone who is willing to go out into the various communities and meet with local officials, with the local citizen groups, and find out the kinds of concerns they have and take these concerns back to the college and work with the college community to satisfy the needs of the general community." Communication skills mean that the president must be able to mix equally well with blue-collar workers, professional people, politicians, students, and faculty. Finally, one trustee believes the president must communicate effectively "up and down the ladder of the organization," letting the faculty know what is going on with the board and letting the board know what is happening on campus.

Certainly it is no surprise that trustees want a president who can communicate effectively, for no public institution will receive the support it requires unless its mission is understood. Presidents must also communicate effectively with their board members and members of the college community. Yet trustees want more in their presidents than someone who has a vision and communicates effectively.

Leadership in Other Areas. While communicating effectively is an important leadership skill, the ideal president must lead in other areas as well. For example, one trustee believes that "the most important thing is that the president be respected in his field by the people he meets." Similarly, in addition to wanting someone who can deal with the funding system under which the college operates, one trustee wants "someone who is sympathetic to and definitely knows education and how to deal with some of the issues and concerns of our particular geographical location." Another just assumes that the president has "leadership skills, naturally." A pretty big assumption, it should be noted.

"What we look for is somebody who has leadership skills, some management skills, although in that area you can hire someone with expertise" is how one trustee described her ideal president. "We need a person who is outstanding and knowledgeable in his own academic field, a person with good interpersonal skills, a person with physical stamina to hold up to the demands of the job" is another trustee's outlook on the situation.

One trustee believes integrity to be the first criterion for the ideal president, "regardless of style or experience or anything else, for if the individual does not have personal integrity he or she is an unacceptable candidate to lead our institution." One trustee who has been on the governing board for six years, and who has worked with two presidents and one interim president during that time, notes that her board places a high priority on integrity and trust before employing a president. "There has been a lot of care taken in choosing the president, and I think we have selected a person in whom we have the highest confidence as far as ethics and responsibility are concerned."

Vision, communication, trust, and getting along with all segments of the population are important considerations when describing the ideal president. Trustees also know that in order to be effective in these areas, a president must have a thorough understanding of the college's community.

Knowing the Community. Most trustees noted, in one way or another, the ideal president must know the community served by the college. This knowledge includes knowing the political scene as well as the social and economic scenes. As one trustee observes, "We look for someone who knows the demographics, knows the business community, or can quickly get up to speed with the business community's needs, and be able to work with local industry to develop the training necessary to keep people employed and to keep those employed up-to-date on technological changes."

Knowing the community includes knowing its politics and working effectively in the political environment. One trustee, whose college is located in the state capital, believes that political skills are even more important in the case of her college than is generally true elsewhere. As she observes, being in the capital city means that "we are kind of under the spotlight as far as community college education is concerned. Our president needs to have really special skills working with legislators and their staff at all levels, but especially in working with the state legislature."

The trustees of a college that changed from what the trustee refers to as "a vo-tech school" to a community college kept the same individual on as president because the trustees were looking for a president who could follow the directions of the board. The trustees liked him because "he was aware of the political landscape in the community, knew the institution, and he had the support of the faculty." The president also "had an open mind and was pliable enough that he would take directions from the board." As implied throughout this volume, working effectively with the board is a necessity for all successful presidents. The ideal president would certainly have the ability to work with the board as a personal characteristic.

Only three of the trustees interviewed mentioned that the ideal president would be someone who could raise money from sources other than through the political process and student fees. One reason for trustees failing to place major emphasis on fundraising as a function of the ideal president may be that community colleges have not only survived but flourished on local, state, and federal dollars and student fees for a number of years. Another reason may be that community colleges entered the race for private funds rather late compared to much of the rest of higher education; therefore, private fundraising has been a priority for many community colleges only in recent years. Perhaps the most important reason that trustees did not emphasize private fundraising is that, in contrast to trustees at most four-year institutions, the trustees do not see fundraising as a high priority for themselves. As pointed out in chapter 4, trustees rank fundraising last on the list of the activities in which they expend their efforts. In any event, the ideal president must work with the board to obtain the necessary resources for operating the college.

Of the trustees who referred to fundraising as an ability of their ideal president, one noted that raising funds is "a very important part of our particular institution." Another trustee who mentioned fundraising as an important function of the president's office felt that his college needs "someone at the helm" who is a fundraiser and who would work well with the college's foundation "to ensure that the funding coming into our institution outside our normal course of funding remains as high as it can be so that we don't rely only on our reimbursement from the state, local sponsors, and the students."

Another trustee who mentioned fundraising notes, "We get X number of dollars from the state but at the same time we have to be creative and get funding from other sources." One cannot overemphasize the role of the ideal president in obtaining resources for the college; obtaining resources from private sources seems to be an evolving function that is more important in some colleges than in others.

Experience Counts. Nearly three out of every ten current community college presidents have held two or more presidencies (Vaughan & Weisman, 1996). How do trustees feel about selecting a sitting president when seeking their ideal president? One of the trustees interviewed stated specifically that he would seek a president with previous presidential experience: "We would look for, first of all, someone who has been involved as a leader of an institution, as a president, before." This trustee's ideal president, in addition to having prior presidential experience, "would have good rapport with the staff and faculty and would be accepted well by the community."

Although only one of the trustees interviewed referred specifically to selecting a president with prior presidential experience (the question asked about desirable skills and attributes, not experience), this should not be taken to mean that prior presidential experience is unimportant when boards seek presidents. Indeed, when asked on the survey to rank their choices for president from a list of candidates based upon their previous experience, over 75% of the trustees would seek as their first choice for president (as their ideal president) someone with prior presidential experience. Because trustees cannot always get their first choice, they often must turn to someone other than a "sitting" president. Their second choice is a chief academic officer. On the other end of the scale, 61% of the trustees indicated that someone outside the community college or higher education fields would be their last choice, thus suggesting that most trustees are not actively seeking business leaders, military officers, school superintendents, or other individuals from outside the field of higher education when filling a presidency (CTS). It is likely, then, that the ideal president will come from within community college ranks. The choices and their rankings are presented in Figure 7.1.

Selecting the President

The selection of a new president is a major event on most community college campuses. Essentially everyone with an interest in the college—faculty, administrators, staff, students, community leaders, alumni, and others—has an interest in who will be selected. Most governing boards acknowledge the high interest in the presidential selection process and seek the views and recommendations of any number of individuals and groups.

The governing board chairs were asked a number of questions that dealt with the presidential selection process. (Because the chairs were asked to select all choices that apply to their situation, the percentages exceed 100%.) One question asked of the chairs was who participates in establishing the qualifications required for the presidency. Almost 84% of the chairs

Figure 7.1   Trustees' ideal candidate for the presidency

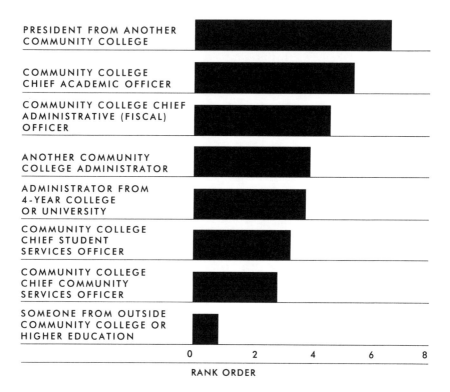

PRESIDENT FROM ANOTHER
COMMUNITY COLLEGE

COMMUNITY COLLEGE
CHIEF ACADEMIC OFFICER

COMMUNITY COLLEGE CHIEF
ADMINISTRATIVE (FISCAL)
OFFICER

ANOTHER COMMUNITY
COLLEGE ADMINISTRATOR

ADMINISTRATOR FROM
4-YEAR COLLEGE
OR UNIVERSITY

COMMUNITY COLLEGE
CHIEF STUDENT
SERVICES OFFICER

COMMUNITY COLLEGE
CHIEF COMMUNITY
SERVICES OFFICER

SOMEONE FROM OUTSIDE
COMMUNITY COLLEGE OR
HIGHER EDUCATION

0   2   4   6   8

RANK ORDER

responded that the governing board participates; over 18% state that the
human resources office participates; over 15% state that community leaders
participate; 14% state that the current president participates; and over 46%
state that the selection advisory committee (the search committee) participates. (As can be seen in Figure 7.2, faculty members serve on the search
committee and, therefore, participate in establishing the qualifications
required for the presidency.) Over 22% use outside consultants in developing the qualifications (CS).

Figure 7.2 Percent of boards involving selected participants in presidential selection

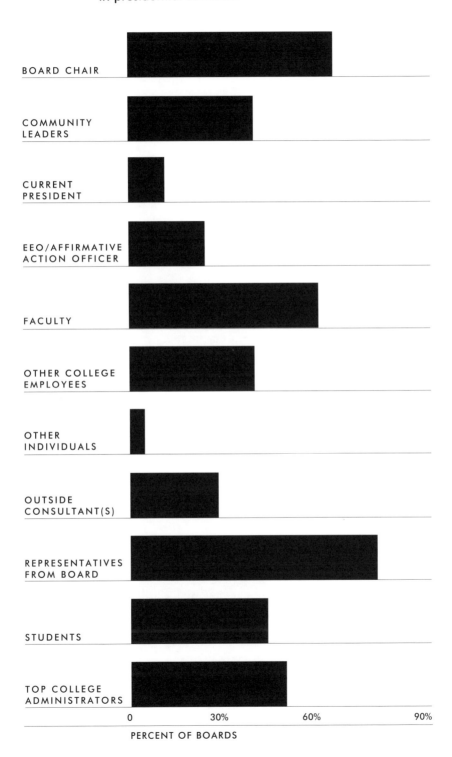

PERCENT OF BOARDS

The chairs were asked which groups or individuals participate on the presidential search committee. Figure 7.2 shows the people or groups whom the chairs identify as serving on the search committee.

Almost 80% of the trustees note that their college advertises presidential vacancies in *The Chronicle of Higher Education* and similar publications. The criteria established for the position are used in rating the applications for the presidency at 72% of the chairs' colleges. Almost 47% of the chairs state that their colleges analyze the application pool to determine if minorities and women are included (CS).

The chairs were asked if the board has a written policy that requires that a woman be on the list of candidates to be interviewed. Four percent of the chairs state that their board has a written policy requiring that a woman be included on that list. Of the 96% of the chairs who answered that their college has no written policy of including a woman on the list of candidates to be interviewed, 18% stated that current practice requires that a woman be on the list of candidates (CS). (A number of the chairs commented on the survey that their board's practice *encourages* but does not *require* including women on the list of candidates to be interviewed.)

The same questions were asked regarding minorities. Over 7% of the chairs responded that their college has a written policy requiring minorities to be on the list of the candidates to be interviewed. Of the 93% of the chairs who responded that their college does not have a written policy on including minorities on the list, 23% of the chairs stated that the current board practice requires the inclusion of minority candidates on the list of candidates to be interviewed (CS). (A number of the chairs commented on the survey that their board's practice *encourages* but does not *require* including minorities on the list of candidates to be interviewed.)

Board chairs were asked who conducts the initial interviews with the presidential candidates. Seventy-two percent of the chairs responding to the survey said that the search committee conducts initial interviews; board members conduct the initial interview at 29% of the colleges represented by the board chairs responding to the survey; 12% involve top-level administrators in the initial interview; over 15% use consultants to conduct the initial interviews (CS). As is shown by the total percentage of those involved in conducting the initial interviews, many boards involve more than one group in the process.

The final question relating to the presidential selection process asked board chairs who conducts the interviews with the finalists for the presidency. Over 42% state that the search committee conducts the final interviews; over 74% state that board members conduct the final interviews; over 16% of the boards involve selected members of the administration; and over 13% state that faculty and staff conduct the final interviews (CS).

Community college governing boards have much help in their search for the perfect president. They also are likely to conduct the presidential search in full public view, for over 33% of the trustees feel that "sunshine practices" are a good way of conducting business; another 62% feel that operating in the "sunshine" is a good idea with some exceptions (CTS).

Even when the presidential search is done in full public view, with the assistance of any number of constituent groups and individuals, the governing board knows that after the talking is over, after all views have been heard, whom to employ as president is the governing board's decision.

So who is the ideal president? The above comments shed light on some things trustees look for in a president. The president should be a leader with vision, with the ability to make the vision a reality, and with the ability to communicate that vision to the various segments of the college and the community. Even though only three trustees mentioned fundraising specifically, trustees fully expect the ideal president to secure the necessary resources for operating the college, whether the resources come through the political process, through the college's foundation, or from working with business and industry. The ideal president would be at ease in most social and political situations, communicating equally well with all segments of the college community and the community at large. The president would know the professional field and understand that the college must be managed well.

One trustee's comment about the type of person needed at his institution summarizes the need for and difficulty in obtaining the ideal president: "Those are pretty big shoes to fill, and you don't necessarily find a man or woman who is great in all areas, but you try to find someone who can work around the strong points and increase his or her awareness where he or she is weak." Of course, the ideal president will work effectively with and provide leadership to the governing board, faculty, staff, and students. And, as one trustee observes, "the ideal president will be somebody who can follow the direction of the board and execute that policy for the betterment of the college." Assuming the presidential candidate possesses all or most of the above characteristics and attributes as well as the others required at a particular college at a certain point in time, given a choice, the great majority of the trustees would select someone with prior presidential experience.

Presidents' Ideal Governing Board

Presidents are somewhat at a disadvantage when discussing their ideal board; while governing boards hire and fire presidents, presidents do not normally select trustees for the governing board. Presidents do, however, have some influence on who is on the college's governing board. As stated previously, over 12% of the trustees said that the major influence on their decision to apply for membership on the governing board came from presidents. Even when presidents do not directly influence trustee selection, they certainly have perceptions regarding what the ideal board would look like. Those presidents interviewed for this study were asked to describe their ideal board. Their perceptions are presented below.

Diversity and Balance. Chapter 5 discussed representation on the governing board from the perspective of both trustees and presidents. The emphasis in that discussion was on the question of whether the board should reflect the makeup of the community that the college serves. The discussion emphasized a balanced board in terms of women and minorities. One perspective presented in that chapter was that a board that reflects the makeup of the community is not always possible. The survey question for those presidents interviewed was not to describe what was possible but rather to describe the ideal board.

One president concludes that "a good board for a community college represents the community. Its members would have diversity in terms of the area they represent such as business, industry, manufacturing, agriculture, and all of those kinds of work-related areas. I think there needs to be diversity in terms of age, in terms of male-female, and I would like to see the board represent the ethnic background of the community as well." Another president wants a balanced board, but he defines balance in ways that differ from the discussion in chapter 5 and from the president quoted above.

> I think that the best fit for a president and a board is to have a board that is very balanced. By balanced, I mean it has a number of perspectives there that represent the real world. I would not want a board that had all public employees, nor would I want a board that had all private business or professional people. I do want a board that has some persons who are public employees, some who are business people—small and large, and a couple of professional people, making recommendations on the basis of where they are coming from and what they bring to the board in terms of their own professional work. That kind of balance reflects what is needed to understand what goes on in a public community college. So many of our colleges do not have that kind of balance. I haven't said anything about representing certain segments of the community ethnically or economically. I don't think that is absolutely critical.

One president wants diversity on his ideal board: "You started off with a good question. Well, I would like a board that pretty much reflects the makeup of the community in terms of gender and racial makeup and probably in terms of socioeconomic elements within the community, with all of them reflected on the board."

Managerial and Leadership Experience. Although trustees and presidents are careful to draw the line between the board's policymaking role and the president's administrative role, presidents nevertheless recognize the value of having trustees on the governing board who understand and appreciate the role and scope of the chief executive officer. Based upon the first author's experience as a president and what he has learned from studying and writing about the community college presidency, most presidents realize that those trustees who have functioned in high-level leadership or managerial positions have little desire or inclination to "micro" manage the college; rather they willingly leave the day-to-day affairs in the hands of the president and staff.

One of the presidents interviewed clearly understands the need to have some trustees who have functioned at the top level of their organization. His ideal board would have "somebody who has been in a managerial position, who understands and has had to deal with some of the top-level managerial issues, because I find that those people tend to have a better understanding of the issues. They are able to have a better balance on decisions and not overreact on certain items that may come before the board because they have been in that seat before and can react to issues with a fairly level head."

Another president would like "board members who understand their respective roles as trustees and the role of the president and, of course, understand the age-old separation of policymaking versus policy implementation. It would be a board that would understand that it has every right to set policy but would then hold the president responsible and accountable for implementing that policy in an equitable and appropriate way."

The chancellor of a large community college district also described the ideal trustee as one who had "been there": "I think I would want trustees to have some credentials in leadership themselves. I find that people who come to the board make the best contribution when they have gone through some of life's enigmas and challenges already." Similarly, another president wants a "board that has some understanding of what the community college is all about and has some understanding of running large institutions."

Knowing the Community and the College Mission. While one expects effective trustees to understand the college's mission and to know a great deal about the community served by the college, three of the presidents interviewed specifically referred to knowing the mission and the community as desirable traits of the ideal trustees. From one president comes the following perspective: "I would, number one, want to have people on the board who had some understanding and were capable of having a good understanding of what the mission of the college is about. I would want people who had connections in the community, both political and civic, and probably economic." From another: "That's a good question. I think I would like primarily people on the board who are highly respected in the community, whatever walks of life they might represent. I don't particularly care whether they are business leaders or whether they are small business people or professionals or what they might be, but I do need people who are experienced community leaders."

Another president describes his ideal board, in part: "I think it would be a board that would understand the mission and the role of a community college." Another president wants "someone who could represent the college in a professional way out in the community, someone who could communicate well, and who would not embarrass the institution." The observations of the presidents quoted above show how important it is that trustees understand the college's mission and the community.

Personal Characteristics and Compatibility. Earlier in this book it was suggested that the board-president relationship was like a marriage in that both entities are entering into what they expect to be a long-term relationship that requires commitment, hard work, and understanding on the part of both parties. Boards and presidents are joined together "for better or worse," if not until death, at least for the near future. With this in mind, presidents look for characteristics in the ideal board that are compatible with their own needs and views. One president is very decisive in expressing his views on what makes for a compatible relationship.

> I would want trustees to be well put together as people, to know who they are, and to have a lot of personal security. If they've raised a family or if they are raising teenagers or whatever, all of those things have a bearing on the effectiveness of board members. They have to know about life and they have to know who they are. I find that's really important. If they are looking for the board to fulfill some particular need like ego or power or influence or they want to use the board to add to themselves, I find that's usually more difficult to deal with than people who want to give service and are interested in the general interworkings of things and have a natural curiosity. It helps if they are really pretty smart, but that doesn't overshadow character.

Another president believes that "it goes without saying that the president certainly has to be able to develop and have a chemistry with the board that enables the president to relate well with the board." From the president of a small rural college comes the following observation about the ideal fit she desires: "Fortunately, I can say the board would look very much like the one I have. I think the fit means there is a similarity in leadership style. I have a very participative leadership style; and if the board did not share that, it would make it very difficult for me to function and for them to understand how I work with the institution. I think a lot of what we might consider fit doesn't happen right from the beginning, but it's something that, like any relationship, people forge over the blacksmith's fire over time. You allow one another to influence each other, and it's important, I think, that the board members and the president both are open to that possibility."

Another president feels that "one of the things a president needs in order to be successful, in order to cause change in an institution, is a courageous board. So I guess I would want board members who are willing to take risks, rational good-sense risks, with their president; someone who would support presidential decisions and strategies even if they might run counter to the prior way things were done."

The following statement from the president of a mid-size college offers observations that provide an apt concluding statement for this section:

Primarily, what I need the board to do is just sort of help me set the general tone and long-time priorities for the college and then to be a very effective sounding board for me. If we are headed in a direction, and people in the community either don't understand what we are doing or are not in agreement with what we are doing, trustees can hear those things and be effective in articulating them to me. As you know from your experience as a president [referring to the first author of this book], people tend to tell college presidents what they think they want to hear. I need people who are so highly respected and have such a good range of contacts in the community that when they come together and say, "Yes, we think we are on track," they are not just expressing their own opinion, that they know we are on track. They are saying, "Yes, we think the majority of the people we serve believe we are on track."

Summary

What do trustees consider to be the ideal match when choosing a president? And what would the presidents' ideal board look like? The above observations shed some light on the subjects. There are, however, other considerations that go into answering the questions.

Although not always addressed specifically in the interviews, the trustees' ideal president would possess many of the attributes and skills identified in other studies. Presidents would exercise good judgment, possess unquestionable integrity, have the courage of his or her convictions, be concerned for others, be flexible, understand and be committed to the community college philosophy, have a sense of humor, be fairly intelligent, and be someone who excels in what he or she does. In addition, the ideal president would readily produce results, select capable people, communicate effectively, resolve conflicts among members of the college community, motivate others, analyze data effectively, take risks (but not too many), and in general have the skills and knowledge required to operate a complex institution effectively (Vaughan, 1986).

As shown in the responses to the trustee surveys, board members want presidents who are responsive and accessible to them. In addition, trustees want presidents with a vision and a plan for achieving their vision; they want presidents who know the community, including the political scene, and have the ability to get along with people from all segments of the community; they want presidents who are accomplished professionals, knowing their field and being respected in that field; they want presidents who can obtain resources and manage them wisely; and, all things considered, trustees' ideal president would have prior presidential experience.

Presidents would like trustees who represent a broad section of the community and who know and understand that community; they want trustees who have experience in top leadership and managerial positions; they want candor in trustees; they want trustees who understand and are committed to the community college mission; and, perhaps most of all, presidents want a board with which they are compatible, including having common goals and approaches to leadership and college governance. And as shown from the presidents' responses, they want board members who are responsive and accessible to the president.

Do trustees find their ideal president? They probably do not. Trustees can, however, take some steps that will move them in the direction of choosing the president they perceive as meeting their standards. One step is to develop a position description that includes the characteristics and skills boards seek in a president. If they want a president adept at working in the political arena, this criterion should be noted in the position announcement. The same is true if they want a president who is committed to diversity among faculty and administrators. Due to the work of the Association of Community College Trustees' CEO Search Service, assisting community college governing boards and search committees across the nation, position vacancy announcements are more comprehensive than they were in the past and the search process has been streamlined. An observation made by a trustee emphasizes the role ACCT plays in presidential searches: "We have just been through the process of selecting a new college president, and this was the second time that I was involved in the process. We went through the Association of Community College Trustees for help this time, and that was quite an experience and in itself very rewarding."

Once the position vacancy announcement is developed and published, it should be the guide for interviewing and selecting the president. For the board to develop a position description and fail to speak to it during the search for a president and to fail to base its selection at least, in part, on the listed criteria, is negligence on the part of the board. It is also unfair to the search committee and to those presidential candidates who have prepared for the interview based upon the published criteria for the position.

Presidents should be prepared to speak to each point in the announcement. If a presidential applicant misleads the board in the interview (expressing a commitment to the board's call for diversity without believing in diversity, for example) and is selected to fill the vacancy, the new president should not be surprised when conflict emerges. Ideally, presidential applicants should feel as free to ask trustees and other members of the presidential search committee (and later in the process, the full board) questions as are trustees and others free to ask the applicant questions. The ideal interview should be more like a conversation that one might engage in when considering entering into any long-term commitment. Unfortunately, too often presidential applicants, especially those seeking their first presidency, are hesitant to ask difficult questions or take a strong stand on what might be a controversial issue during the presidential interview for fear of being eliminated from consideration for the position.

In summary, if trustees are going to find their ideal president and if potential presidents are going to find that "match made in heaven" in their governing board, much of the courting must take place prior to the day the agreement is made final; when the president begins work, it may be too late to correct many misconceptions. Trustees must take the lead in assuring that they know what they are seeking in a president, be candid in their expectations, and base their selection on the criteria they deem desirable. Potential presidents must understand that the board is seeking an individual with certain personal attributes and leadership skills and be prepared to bring those attributes and skills to the boardroom table and to use them in achieving the college's mission. Approaching the process in this manner will not assure the perfect match; it will, however, assure that all of the players understand and play by the rules of the game.

Enhancing the Trustees' Role

The preceding chapters examine the community college trustee's role from a number of perspectives. All evidence up to this point indicates that trustees take their role seriously, bringing to it energy, commitment, understanding, knowledge, and, in many cases, love and passion.

What has not been examined up to this point is how trustees improve their own knowledge and performance, assess themselves, or engage in professional development and related activities. This chapter examines some of those influences and activities that enhance the trustee's role. The concluding section offers suggestions on how community college governing boards can improve their effectiveness. The perspectives of both trustees and presidents are considered in this examination.

Board Expectations for Itself. Many of the quotes from trustees in the preceding chapters contain elements of both humility and confidence. For example, the trustee who feels both "big and small" at graduation knowing what the community college means to so many individuals and from knowing that the governing board played a role in serving those individuals, displays both confidence and humility. Most trustees are also successful people who have high expectations for themselves. Do these expectations transfer to their roles as trustees?

Trustees were asked to rate how clear and realistic their board's expectations are. Over 81% of the 609 trustees responding to the question rate the expectations of the board as clear and realistic; 1.8% perceive the expectations to be clear but unrealistic; and over 16% perceive the expectations to be unclear (CTS).

Presidents were also asked to rate how they perceive the governing board's expectations of itself. Over 76% of the presidents perceive the board's expectations to be clear and realistic; 1.7% perceive the expectations to be clear but unrealistic; and 22% of the presidents perceive the board's expectations of itself to be unclear (PS).

One can conclude that, in general, governing boards have clear and realistic expectations of themselves in the great majority of the cases. On the other hand, one can also conclude that work needs to be done with many boards to make sure that all members know and understand what is expected of their boards.

Board Goals. Expectations often manifest themselves through goals. As noted on a number of occasions in this book, trustees pride themselves on setting goals or outcomes for their boards and their colleges. A survey question asked the trustees if the board's goals were clear. Over 49% of the trustees responding stated that the goals are very clear; over 36% perceive the goals to be somewhat clear; and over 14% feel the goals are not very clear or not clear at all (CTS).

Presidents were asked their perception of how clear the board's goals are. Almost 41% of the presidents perceive the goals to be very clear; over 43%

of the presidents perceive the goals to be somewhat clear; and over 16% feel that the board's goals are not very clear or not clear at all (PS).

Goal setting and goal clarification is an ongoing, tedious process requiring much time and energy. Based upon the results of the surveys, a number of boards could profit from spending more time and energy clarifying their goals.

Planning for the College's Welfare. How well do trustees plan for the long-term welfare of their community colleges? This question was asked of those trustees receiving the trustees' survey. Over 83% of the trustees responding to the survey (613 responded) rated the long-term planning to be excellent or good; over 15% perceive the planning to be fair or poor; and 1.6% of the trustees (10 trustees) believe that there is no long-term planning taken by trustees for the welfare of the institution (CTS).

Presidents were asked how they rate the board's planning for the overall welfare of the college. Over 80% of the 298 presidents responding to the question perceive the planning to be excellent or good; over 17% believe it to be fair or poor; and 2.3% (seven presidents) perceive that no planning for the long-term welfare of the institution takes place by the board (PS).

Over 80% of the trustees and presidents rate the overall long-term planning the board engages in to be excellent or good.

Managing Finances. Anyone who understands the board's role in setting policies and the president's role in carrying out the policies knows that the board does not manage the college's finances on a day-to-day basis. (Nor do presidents, for that matter.) On the other hand, the governing board has the responsibility to see that the institution's finances are managed effectively, efficiently, and responsibly, a responsibility which includes approving capital outlay and operating budgets. A survey question asked trustees how they would rate the board's guidance for managing the college's finances. Almost 87% of the trustees view the board's guidance as excellent or good; 13% view the guidance as fair to poor; and less than 1% (3 trustees out of 614) view the board's guidance for managing the college's finances as nonexistent (CTS).

Presidents were asked to rate the guidance their boards give in managing the college's finances. Matching the trustees, almost 87% of the presidents rate the guidance as excellent or good; over 12% rate the guidance as fair to poor; and less than 1% (2 presidents out of 299) rate the guidance given by the board in managing the college's finances as nonexistent (PS).

Trustees and presidents perceive that the governing board offers excellent or good guidance for managing the college's finances. Good financial management is a necessity for the successful community college. Based on the survey results, trustees and presidents realize that assuring that the college engages in good financial practices is a critical part of the governing board's role.

Board Assessment

An often difficult task facing community college governing boards is assessing their own effectiveness. Assessment may be formal or informal; it may be accomplished with the help of an outside consultant or by the board members themselves; board assessment may or may not involve the college president, faculty, and other members of the college community. In any event, assessing its own performance is something a board must do if it is to understand and fulfill its role effectively.

The trustees interviewed were asked if their board engaged in self-evaluation and, if so, what process they followed. In addition to the interviews, the chair and non-chair trustee surveys asked questions on board assessment, as did the president's survey. The following observations on board assessment provide insights into this important process.

Formal Assessment. Board chairs were asked if their board undergoes a formal assessment of its practices and, if so, how often the formal assessment takes place. Slightly more than half (50.8%) of the board chairs stated that their board has a formal assessment of its practices. The remaining 49% have no formal board assessment (CS).

Of those 87 boards that have formal assessments, 31% use outside consultants in the process, whereas 77% conduct a formal assessment without an outside consultant. (Seven chairs—8%—responded that their board conducts formal assessments both with and without outside consultants.) Of the 87 boards that conduct a formal assessment, over 71% conduct a formal assessment every year; almost 7% conduct the assessment every other year; 2.7% conduct it every three years; and the remaining 19% have no regular schedule for conducting a formal assessment of its board (CS).

The board chairs were asked what areas and functions their boards assess when doing a formal assessment. Figure 8.1 lists some of the areas assessed and shows the percentage of boards assessing each area.

Figure 8.1 Areas included in board assessment

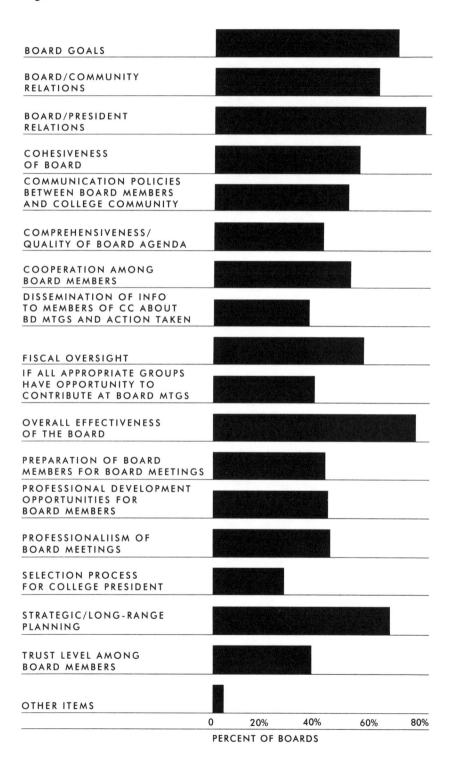

BOARD GOALS

BOARD/COMMUNITY
RELATIONS

BOARD/PRESIDENT
RELATIONS

COHESIVENESS
OF BOARD

COMMUNICATION POLICIES
BETWEEN BOARD MEMBERS
AND COLLEGE COMMUNITY

COMPREHENSIVENESS/
QUALITY OF BOARD AGENDA

COOPERATION AMONG
BOARD MEMBERS

DISSEMINATION OF INFO
TO MEMBERS OF CC ABOUT
BD MTGS AND ACTION TAKEN

FISCAL OVERSIGHT

IF ALL APPROPRIATE GROUPS
HAVE OPPORTUNITY TO
CONTRIBUTE AT BOARD MTGS

OVERALL EFFECTIVENESS
OF THE BOARD

PREPARATION OF BOARD
MEMBERS FOR BOARD MEETINGS

PROFESSIONAL DEVELOPMENT
OPPORTUNITIES FOR
BOARD MEMBERS

PROFESSIONALIISM OF
BOARD MEETINGS

SELECTION PROCESS
FOR COLLEGE PRESIDENT

STRATEGIC/LONG-RANGE
PLANNING

TRUST LEVEL AMONG
BOARD MEMBERS

OTHER ITEMS

0   20%   40%   60%   80%

PERCENT OF BOARDS

Board chairs were also asked who participates in formal board assessment. The chairs were given a list of potential participants and were asked to circle all that apply; thus the total exceeds 100%. Figure 8.2 illustrates who participates in formal assessment of the board (CS).

The last question on formal assessment asked of the board chairs related to the dissemination of the results of board assessments. The recipients of the results are shown in Figure 8.3 (CS). Again, the chairs were given a list of

Figure 8.2   Percent of boards involving selected participants in formal board assessment

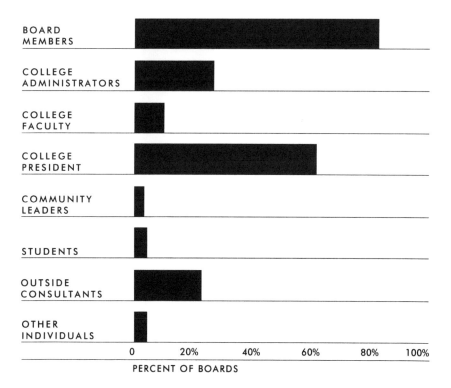

169

Figure 8.3 Percent of boards that distribute the results of
board assessment to selected groups

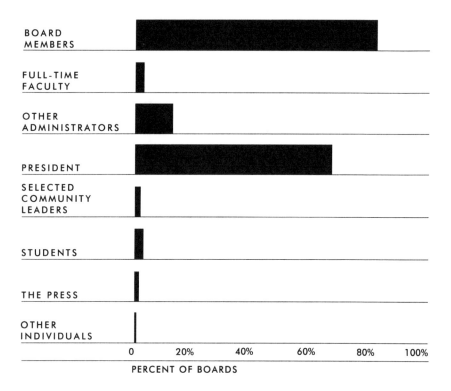

potential recipients of the formal assessment and were asked to circle all that apply; thus the total exceeds 100%.

Assessment as a Communication Tool. Although the dissemination of the results of the board's formal evaluation is limited to a select audience, trustees nevertheless feel that board assessment, whether formal or informal, is valuable in communicating its role to members of the college community and the public. Eighty-nine percent of the 596 trustees responding to the question believe that board assessment is very valuable or somewhat valuable in communicating the board's role to its constituents (CTS). Similarly, 88% of the 288 presidents responding to the question view board assessment as very valuable or somewhat valuable in communicating the board's role to the public and members of the college community (PS).

Trustees and presidents perceive board assessment as being helpful in setting the college's agenda for the future. Indeed, 89% of the trustees and 87% of the presidents perceive board assessment as very valuable or valuable in setting the college agenda for the future (CTS; PS).

Board assessment, both formal and informal, is perceived by most trustees and presidents to be important and useful in understanding and communicating the board's role to the public, as well as to members of the college community. This information may demand more attention from trustees and presidents, especially if no dissemination plan currently exists.

Observations on Board Assessment. Those trustees interviewed were asked if their boards engaged in self-assessment and, if so, to comment on the process. The following are their observations.

One trustee notes that "once a year we have a trustee self-evaluation form that we send out to all trustees. It can either be mailed back anonymously or they can put their name on it. We use it as a tool. We have two retreats a year; one deals with the long-range plans, mission, and goals of the institution. The other is what we call a mini-retreat which is based on trustee relationships." Another trustee observes, "What we have is a form that we go through each year that has a list of categories of things we want to know—

whether the board is meeting the community and whether the board is keeping up on things and going to educational meetings. We each have our own separate goals that we set each year, and so we go back and visit them and see if we have really worked on them. This is something new to our board, so we are just kind of working through it now."

Another trustee's answer illustrates the seriousness with which his board approaches the assessment of its role.

> Yes. Annually we do an assessment. We try to have the evaluation at a board workshop. We have five or six of those a year where the board gets together to discuss issues more in depth. We do a board evaluation at those workshops. We went to a company . . . and had them evaluate the type of members we were. It was a psychological-type of test to tell us whether we were introverts, extroverts, and how we can function better in making board decisions. We try to help the board make better decisions by working as a team. We ask, "Do we attend board meetings? Do we contribute to the conversation?" And we just kind of discuss the board's role as a whole.

From another trustee comes this statement about self-assessment: "What we do, we set our goals for the year and determine what we want to see happen with ourselves and in the district. Also, the chancellor prepares his or her goals once a year on what he or she wants to accomplish throughout the year. And at mid-year we look to see if we are going in that direction. At the end of the year we look again. In those areas where we feel we have not accomplished what we wanted, we assess why not. Mid-term assessment allows us to change goals. They are not in concrete."

One trustee notes that although his board does not do a formal evaluation, self-analysis is an ongoing process with his board. "I have yet to find anyone on our board, and I've been on the board five years, who has not sat down with another person and said, 'Why did you make that decision?' This year we have three new board members. Each older board member becomes a mentor to the new board members. So I guess we do a self-evaluation; the self-analysis and critique by other board members is an ongoing process."

Another trustee notes that "every time we do a presidential evaluation it is also an evaluation of the board itself. It is like any other evaluation: it has to be a two-way street. We try to have very candid discussions with the president about where we might improve in what we do also."

The candor of trustees in the interviews is evident (and refreshing). One trustee notes that self-assessment is "the retreat topic. We decided we wouldn't evaluate ourselves as individuals or would not evaluate each other as individuals, but we would look at what has been on our agenda for the last six months and ask ourselves did we do what we should have done. Are we sticking to policy issues? And I can tell you we are not perfect."

Another trustee comments, "Actually we don't [have a formal self-assessment]. No, we don't, and yes, we do. We will sit down during a board retreat. But what I was comparing it to was the local hospital board I chair. We [the hospital board] do a rather detailed self-evaluation."

Another trustee confesses that self assessment is "one of the weaknesses that this current board has in that we have never had a self-evaluation process implemented. It has been discussed on several occasions but the majority of the board has never voted to go along with a self-evaluation process." Another trustee notes, "Well, I don't know that in the six years I've been on the board that we've done a formal evaluation. We've evaluated the president. I think every time we have a retreat we evaluate ourselves informally. We talk about what we have done. We talk about the goals that we set the last time and whether they are still our goals. We talk about our relationship with the president and with the faculty. I think we do evaluate informally, but I don't think we've ever put it on our agenda as a formal item."

From another trustee comes the following observations: "We don't do a formal self-evaluation. We have had ACCT facilitators come to conduct retreats for us, and they have had an instrument for us to evaluate ourselves. When we have retreats—we have one a year—we do a lot of evaluating of ourselves as a board." Similarly, another trustee observes: "What we do mainly is to look at ourselves and we ask our president to evaluate us, to give us some feedback. We talk about if there is a problem; we talk about how we could function better. So we do a self-evaluation of how we are functioning, can it be better, and it could always be better. We ask what kind of steps do we need to take to make it better."

One trustee notes, "Yes, we have an extensive self-evaluation. It is a written document. We discuss the responses that each of us gives on the written document and then see what we can do to improve. We have a retreat every year in which we establish the board goals for the year." Another trustee responds, "Yes, we do formal self-assessment. The board has a retreat at least once a year. The board is looking at an instrument that would allow us to evaluate ourselves after each meeting. A rather quick checklist evaluating how the board is doing. It would be like five points to consider."

Based upon the interviews, trustees approach self-assessment through a number of avenues, some formal and others informal. The board retreat is an important vehicle for self-evaluation.

Professional Activities

In addition to attending board retreats, trustees engage in a number of other activities designed to improve their effectiveness as board members. These activities range from attending national, regional, and state conferences to reading material related to their role as board members. The following sections discuss some of the professional activities engaged in by trustees.

Conventions and Conferences. A survey question asked trustees if they participate in professional development activities related to their duties as board members; over 85% of the trustees reported that they do (CTS). Trustees are also encouraged by presidents to engage in professional development activities. Over 72% of the presidents state that they regularly encourage board members to attend national conventions; another 22% of the presidents occasionally encourage trustees to attend national conferences (PS).

Trustees were asked which conferences and conventions they attend. Figure 8.4 summarizes the trustees' attendance at conferences and conventions. Because some trustees attend more than one conference or convention, the

Figure 8.4   Trustee attendance at conferences and
conventions

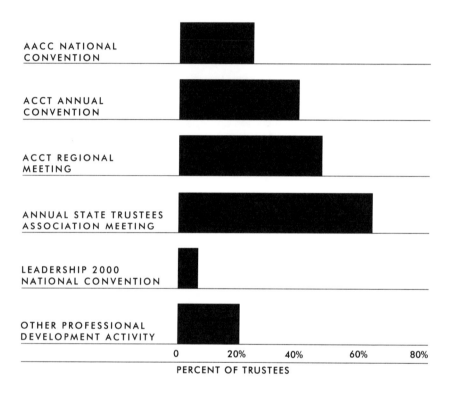

number of trustees attending them exceeds the total of 537 trustees responding to the question. For the same reason, the percentage of trustees attending the various meetings exceeds 100%.

As can be seen from Figure 8.4, the most popular professional meeting trustees attend is their state association's annual meeting. The annual and regional conferences of ACCT are popular among trustees. Many also attend the annual convention of the American Association of Community Colleges.

National Associations. The Association of Community College Trustees (ACCT) and the American Association of Community Colleges (AACC) are the two most important national organizations devoted to understanding and promoting the nation's community colleges. ACCT and AACC jointly sponsor the Community College National Legislative Seminar in Washington, D.C., each February.

ACCT is devoted to serving and representing community college trustees, although presidents also attend its conferences and read and contribute to its literature. ACCT's conferences include an annual convention and annual regional seminars. In addition, ACCT encourages trustees to be active in the associations in their own states. ACCT issues a number of publications, including *Trustee Quarterly* and the bimonthly *Advisor*. ACCT also offers books, monographs, videotapes, a World Wide Web site, teleconferences, and on-site workshops for individual boards to assist trustees in understanding and performing their duties.

During the interviews, trustees were asked to comment on the role of ACCT and other professional associations. One trustee feels that "with any position comes training and ongoing education. If you do not attend state and ACCT meetings, you are not doing your job as a trustee." He notes that he and other members of the board read the literature and that he "is very comfortable with everything that is printed by ACCT." Another trustee feels that it is very important that every member of her board should be involved with the state trustee organization as well as ACCT but acknowledges that it "is sometimes one of the hardest things to do, to get trustees involved at the state and national levels."

Another trustee acknowledges the important role both ACCT and AACC play in working on legislative issues. She is grateful that the organizations have full-time staff members devoted to working with members of Congress. One trustee finds that national meetings serve as "a sounding board for what other people are doing and in keeping abreast of what the issues are in community colleges." While admitting that he does not read as much of the literature published by ACCT and AACC as he should, he nevertheless feels it is extremely valuable, especially to new trustees. Another trustee feels that ACCT and AACC keep trustees "posted on national issues. Specifically, we pay our dues to participate in those associations so that they can do the tracking and monitoring and lobbying work for us and inform us as a college specifically when we need to take an active role. So certainly those two groups kind of serve as spokes to the hub of the wagon wheel of which we consider ourselves to be the hub."

One trustee values ACCT's educational program: "I think ACCT does an excellent job. I think the annual legislative conference is tremendously important and successful in helping board members know what is going on at the federal level. I think their education [recognition] program—I have completed levels 1 and 2—is an excellent means of helping me focus on skills and issues that make me a better trustee."

Based on the interviews, trustees are sensitive to the need to move beyond the provincialism of the local campus. One trustee believes ACCT and AACC are important because they help trustees understand that "their role extends beyond their own local campus if they are really going to be effective." In a similar view, a trustee believes that ACCT "provides a forum at which trustees can shed some of their provincialism and pick up common experiences that all college trustees deal with." Another comments on the need for trustees to move beyond their own campus in their thinking. "ACCT and AACC are absolutely vital. They are as important as can be, otherwise we would be a number of isolated boards that are inward looking, never having contact with other boards, never getting a broader education on national issues."

One trustee notes, "It is mandatory that we each attend at least one [professional] meeting for our education. They keep the trustee up to snuff. You can read the *Chronicle*, but it is still not like being there and talking. That makes a big difference." A trustee who just completed a term on the board of her state's trustee association finds the literature published by ACCT to be very helpful and notes that she has "been greatly dependent on ACCT to help me figure out what it is I am supposed to be doing and how I can do it best." Another trustee sums up her views rather dramatically on the roles played by ACCT and AACC. "I think that without them, we would be doomed."

Another trustee finds that "the main things they do are the publications and meetings. If you read the publications and attend as many of the meetings as you can, I think you are going to be more effective because you are going to know more and get a wider view than just your own board." A final comment from a board chair expresses the value of ACCT and AACC to his board: "Well, I think they play a tremendous role. First of all, they are kind of our home office. They are where we operate, where we get our knowledge, our information on how to be better trustees. They are a kind of think tank for us. They have very good publications. The more articles they do from other areas across the country the more it helps us, because we pick up things out of those articles."

Based upon the interviews, trustees place a high value on the roles played by national organizations. Especially important is the literature published by ACCT and AACC and the various conferences and conventions these organizations sponsor.

Suggestions for Improving Board Operations

Those trustees and presidents interviewed were asked to suggest ways in which community college governing boards could improve their performance. The following are summaries of the suggestions offered by the trustees who participated in the interviews. As the reader will discover, most of the suggestions for improving board performance reaffirm and build upon many of the things that trustees are already doing.

Education. The most persistent suggestion emanating from the interviews is that boards should continue and intensify their educational development. The following comments on how to improve board effectiveness come from three trustees:

Well, I think number one to improving board effectiveness is education. Board members need to be better educated on what their roles and responsibilities are.

Continue with the education of the board as to what is expected of them, what their duties are, and offer opportunities to learn about those sort of things.

To improve board effectiveness, trustees have to be educated about their role.

Another suggestion falls under the education umbrella and serves to illustrate one form trustee education might take: trustees should attend their association meetings at the state, regional, and national levels. The following comments from trustees endorse this attendance:

Trustees have to attend meetings that are specifically designed to help trustees be more effective. Attending their state meetings; attending regional meetings; attending ACCT meetings.

To improve effectiveness we need to attend meetings like FACC [Florida Association of Community Colleges] and the regional meetings and ACCT meetings. I think they help us to become better at what we do.

Communication. Just as one would expect education to show up on any list of activities required to improve the operation of a governing board, it is not surprising that trustees returned to one of their favorite themes—effective communication—when offering suggestions on improving board effectiveness. The following comment illustrates what one trustee (obviously not from a "sunshine" state) thinks about communication as a means of improving board effectiveness. "Fellow board members and the president have got to work in harmony. Board members need to keep in the board meetings exactly what is going on there. There should be no leaks."

A special form of communication is used when reaching consensus on issues. One trustee feels that "one thing we could do to improve board effectiveness is to provide more training to trustees on reaching consensus." Another trustee comments, "I think that communication between the board members and the president and the college as a whole is extremely important." A president suggests that there exists a "kind of nebulous relationship between the board and the president" that can be cleared up through communication. He notes that "the old homily about boards dealing with policy and presidents dealing with administration" does not always hold. "There are a lot of things that are neither fish nor fowl; they are both." His solution is that boards and president talk about what is policy and what is administration in order to avoid crossing the boundaries between policy and administration.

Board Operations. A third area in which trustees and presidents believe improvements in the board's effectiveness can occur is in board activities and functions. One trustee believes that one "way trustees can be effective is by making sure that they understand the vision of their community college and that all things they do are guided by that vision and the mission of the college." Another trustee comments, "Number one, make sure that you are doing what your board ought to be doing and that you are not spending time rubber-stamping what the college is already doing." Another trustee believes board improvement can be accomplished if trustees "keep focusing on the ends they want to achieve and, in our case, always tie them back to that long-range plan that is not so long because we do it every year."

A president suggests, "The first step, I would think, is setting some goals, like the college has goals, the president has goals, and the staff has goals. I think the board should have some annual goals it wants to achieve in helping to move the college to its vision. I think obviously that some kind of assessment would be helpful." Another president suggests that what is needed is for his board to "establish a system that all can buy into, so there is an understanding across the board and across the institution of what the expectations are and how they will be evaluated."

Another president believes that "if the board could get focused on the ends and not the means, I think we could start a revolution at a place like this. A lot of people grasp 'policy governance' and then when they try to implement it they have a lot of trouble." Another president perceives that trustees at his institution "really never learn enough about the college. They don't have a sense about the college; they come to the institution at night; they don't necessarily see the students; they don't necessarily see the hustle and bustle of the campus; they don't know the programs that are going on although we share information with them."

Any number of other suggestions came from trustees and presidents, including the need for the board to engage in self-evaluation. One trustee suggests, "One step that could be taken to improve board effectiveness is to implement a self-evaluation process." A president notes, "We haven't gotten to it yet, but I think a self-evaluation of the board would improve its effectiveness." Another president believes it is important that trustees be fully oriented to their role: "I think this requires attending ACCT meetings and learning what other trustees think about community college issues, and I think that includes self-evaluation." Other suggestions made centered around trustees preparing for board meetings, attending those meetings, becoming more efficient, and in general doing those things one would normally expect of committed and knowledgeable trustees.

A final suggestion in the "general category" for improving the effectiveness of community college governing boards comes from a trustee: "The main thing is to treat your board members . . . as busy people. Keep the information brief, concise, and let them know what questions are going to be posed at the next meeting so they can do their background searches on how they want to vote."

The research on which this chapter is based confirms what most trustees already know: enhancing their effectiveness as board members is an important aspect of being a competent trustee. To be effective, any program of improvement must be comprehensive and ongoing. As the answers to the survey questions and comments from the interviews confirm, being an effective board member means having realistic expectations of the board's role and clearly stating those expectations in the form of goals that can be measured.

This research confirms that if boards are to improve their effectiveness, they must engage in self-assessment, either formal or informal, and the research also confirms and illustrates the importance of educational programs in enhancing the governing board's effectiveness.

Observations, Recommendations, and Issues

Community college trustees are important people. Thus began chapter 1 of this volume. The eight chapters that followed the opening sentence described the role of the women and men who serve on the governing boards of the nation's community colleges.

The first chapter placed these governing boards within the context of American higher education, suggesting that community college trustees contribute to and extend the heritage of lay board leadership of the nation's colleges and universities. The remaining chapters described who the trustees are in terms of gender, race, ethnicity, educational level, and other demographic characteristics. Also described are their relationships with community college presidents, community members, and each other, as well as the satisfactions trustees get from serving on their governing boards. A look was taken at what trustees might seek in their "perfect" president. Also examined are ways trustees can enhance their roles. What observations and recommendations can be made about those individuals who serve on the nation's community college governing boards? What are the issues facing community college boards based upon the information gained from this study? This chapter concludes this examination of community college trustees by addressing these important questions.

Observations and Recommendations

Observation. The first (and perhaps most important) observation is that community college governing boards are made up of individuals who are committed to and enjoy serving on their governing boards. The hundreds of comments returned with the trustees' surveys revealed that they reap enormous satisfaction from their service on the board.

Recommendation. This aspect of trusteeship should be celebrated. Although it is not unusual to hear trustees commiserate with each other about budget constraints, political pressures, and crisis situations, it should be *more* common to hear trustees share with each other, the college community, and the greater community the rewards of serving on a community college board. Such celebratory communication enhances board members' experiences, interests others from the community in becoming involved with college or board activities, and projects a positive image of the community college to the community.

Observation. Trustees are committed to pursuing educational programs that improve their performance and their understanding of the community college's mission. Important in the educational process are state and national trustee associations. Especially important in contributing to the education of trustees is the Association of Community College Trustees. Its national and regional conferences and seminars, literature, and training programs serve as important avenues for trustee training and education. Yet, in spite of the emphasis boards place on education as the avenue through which trustees learn about their role and improve their performance, new trustee orientation is not always conducted. Over 16% of the board chairs state that new board members receive no formal orientation when joining the board.

Recommendation. If trustees are to understand their role and fulfill that role effectively, they must understand the college they have been chosen to govern and understand how they as trustees fit into the college's total governing process. A first step in understanding their role and their college is participation in a formal orientation program. All governing boards should have a formal orientation program for new trustees. The orientations should be conducted by the board chair and the president who would call upon other trustees and staff members to assist in the orientation as needed. Consideration should be given to making the orientation mandatory. (Only 14% of the board chairs stated that their board requires that new trustees attend a formal orientation.) The orientation program should introduce the new trustee to the many facets of the college's operation and the trustee's relationship to the college's operation. *Major* emphasis should be placed on the community college's mission, for no trustee should begin a term on the board without a good understanding of the college's mission. Moreover, the orientation should introduce the new trustee to the literature on the community college, including that produced by ACCT and AACC.

The importance of state, regional, and national meetings should be discussed during the formal orientation. Special emphasis should be placed on participating in ongoing educational programs such as those sponsored by ACCT. To fail to have a formal orientation program for new trustees is to miss a rare opportunity to get these trustees started on the right track.

Observation. One finding that bodes well for the future of community colleges is the degree to which trustees and presidents agree on the many facets of community college trusteeship. Trustees and presidents work well as a team; yet there are a few areas where they disagree (how much time trustees spend or should spend on campus, for example). Both trustees and presidents are sensitive to their respective roles as policymakers and policy implementers. Mutual support and mutual trust is perceived to be strong by both trustees and presidents. Trustees rely heavily upon presidents for information, staff support, and leadership; presidents, in turn, rely upon trustees for guidance and support.

Recommendation. Whereas trustees are sensitive to their role in making policy, there is a temptation on the part of some trustees to move into the daily affairs of the college. Governing boards must maintain constant vigilance against permitting this to happen. Just as importantly, trustees must guard against presidents who move into the policymaking realm.

Among the myriad of strategies that trustees and presidents can use to implement and maintain the separation of roles, two approaches are fundamental and essential: First, trustees and presidents should collaborate on establishing operational parameters for policymaking and administration. Ideally, trustees and presidents should work together to establish consensus on where the line is drawn between policymaking and administration.

Second, trustees and presidents should maintain an open and honest relationship with each other. Because every situation is different and presents unique factors, ongoing dialogue about the distinction between policymaking and administration should occur. In addition, trustees and presidents alike should be allowed and expected to voice their concerns and clarify their understanding of actions that have occurred.

Observation. Based upon the interviews with trustees and presidents, trustees are somewhat unclear on their role in developing the board agenda and establishing priorities for their own operations. This is a tentative observation that requires more study.

Recommendation. The issue of how the board goes about doing its business should be explored further. All trustees should read *A New Vision of Board Leadership* by Carver and Mayhew. This book will provide trustees with a different perspective on the role and responsibility of the governing board and will assist trustees in establishing priorities, regardless of whether they recommend that their college board adopt the "policy governance" model.

Observation. Approximately 16% of the trustees communicate directly with faculty members without the involvement, or even the knowledge, of the president. Some boards may fall back on the old political saw, "If ain't broke, don't fix it." Nevertheless, trustees may find it difficult to stay out of the day-to-day operation of the college if they bypass the president when communicating with the faculty and staff.

Recommendation. When a policy question or an administrative issue or problem is involved, all board communication with the faculty should occur with the president's knowledge, support, and, when appropriate, involvement. Again, formal board communication procedures should be developed and agreed upon jointly between the board and the president. Trustees should be consistent in their interactions with faculty and staff so that everyone is encouraged to use the agreed upon channels of communication. On the other hand, trustees should take every available opportunity to attend college ceremonies, social functions, and other activities that bring them in touch with the faculty and college. At these events, board members' conversations with the faculty should be friendly, open, warm, and devoid of policy questions and faculty problems.

Observation. Without doubt, trustees know for whom they work and whom they represent. Without exception, trustees know that they represent the members of their communities and hold the college in trust on behalf of the people. Trustees express a strong desire to communicate the goals of the college to the people in the college's service area.

Recommendation. The interviews clearly demonstrate that trustees feel strongly about representing the entire community. Careful consideration should be given to *how* and *where* formal communications from the college and board are distributed to the community. All segments of the population within the college's service area must be reached and heard from in order to complete the communication loop between members of the college board and members of the community.

Observation. Those trustees interviewed feel that governing boards should reflect the composition of the communities and student populations the college serves in terms of female and minority representation on the board. A review of the demographic characteristics of current trustees nationwide indicates that the board composition considered ideal by the trustees interviewed is a long way from reality.

Recommendation. Board composition is something that should be approached carefully and thoughtfully. The question that must be asked and answered is whether any given governing board at any given point in time represents the college's service area. If the answer is "yes," then there may be no reason to tamper with the board's current composition. If the answer is "no," board members must ask themselves what can be done to correct the situation.

Boards can take steps to increase diversity among their members. For example, in those cases where the board chooses a replacement for an unexpired term, the vacancy could be filled by a member of an under-represented group. Current board members can also identify a pool of minorities and women who are potential board members. Where the trustees are appointed, the board should share information on potential minority and female candidates with the appointing authorities. Where trustees are elected, potential minority and female candidates can be encouraged to run for the board.

The great majority of governing boards, regardless of their current composition, aim to represent their communities well; nevertheless, current board members should not ignore the value of diversity. The increasing numbers of minority students need role models. In addition, the college needs to assure that it represents all segments of the community. Often this requires a physical presence, especially if equal representation is to have meaning to those from minority groups.

Observation. Trustees know the characteristics and skills they value in a president.

Recommendation. As trustees embark on the presidential selection process, it is important for them to keep in mind that characteristics (such as being visionary and trustworthy) and skills (such as "getting the job done" and communicating effectively) can be developed and demonstrated in a variety of ways. As community colleges face the 21st century, governing boards and presidents will be challenged to assess situations from multiple perspectives. When selecting a new president, trustees should avoid preconceived notions about what the perfect president looks like or how someone becomes a perfect president and should select the candidate that best fits the current and future needs of the college and the community.

Trustees should know how satisfied (or dissatisfied) they are with their current president and why they feel as they do. This knowledge should be gained through presidential evaluations that have measurable objectives as the criteria upon which the evaluation is based. The criteria for presidential evaluation should be clearly understood by all trustees and should be clearly communicated to the president. The major purpose of the formal evaluation process should be to improve presidential performance.

A variety of factors influence a board's decision to dismiss a president and, therefore, boards should move cautiously when contemplating this action. Board members should understand the obstacles they face if they decide to dismiss a president. They should also understand the seriousness of letting a president go, including being aware of the time, expense and, at times, trauma associated with finding a replacement. Nevertheless, if the evaluation reveals that the current president is ineffective, the board has an obligation to seek a replacement.

Observation. The majority of trustees perceive the expectations for their board to be clear and realistic. The same is true regarding their perceptions of their boards' goals. On the other hand, over 16% of the trustees perceive their boards' expectations to be unclear, and over 14% of the trustees perceive their boards' goals to be unclear. Along with these statistics comes the information that 51% of the board chairs responding to the question on formal board assessment state that their board conducts a formal assessment of its performance. (Forty-nine percent of the board chairs state that their boards have no formal plan for assessing their performance.) Far too few boards have formal assessments of board goals and performance.

Recommendation. All trustees should understand what is expected of their board and have a clear understanding of the board's goals. All board members should be involved in developing board expectations and goals. The expectations and goals should be stated clearly and shared with new trustees during orientation. One way of assuring that trustees have a clear understanding of the board's goals and expectations is through self-assessment. All boards should consider a formal assessment plan to determine how well their members understand and fulfill the expectations and goals of the board.

Issues Facing the Community College

The trustees and presidents interviewed for this study were asked to identify the major issue facing the community college in the next four or five years. They were also asked what they, as trustees and presidents, could do to prepare the college to face that issue. The following sections summarize the issues mentioned and some recommendations for dealing with them.

Funding. It will not come as a surprise to anyone who has more than a passing knowledge of the community college to learn that obtaining adequate resources for the college's operation is perceived to be a major issue facing the community college both now and in the future. One trustee observes that "the major issue comes down to funding. Without adequate funding, there are going to be missed opportunities by your community college." Similar comments from trustees follow:

Financing is the major issue now and, I guess, five years from now and 100 years from now.

One of the most important things is the dollars for education and making education accessible.

Not a hard question: it is money.

Funding is going to be one of the most critical issues. It provides equipment, determines what kind of faculty you have, and what kind of facilities you have.

One president observes that the major issue is "clearly, finance. We see in Washington the reduction in funding for education and further restrictions on financial aid. We see the same thing going on in our state." Another president believes that "remaining financially sound is the major issue community colleges must deal with."

Certainly obtaining adequate funding for the community college will be a major issue in the future, just as it has been in the past. In the past, however, funding came more freely than it does today, especially from state legislatures. Moreover, the competition for resources among education, health care, crime control, and other areas has intensified.

Technology and Change. A trustee notes that "the technology is changing every minute, and we must be prepared to deal with that and upgrade our technology and training or we are going to be behind times with someone coming out of our college [with training on obsolete systems]." Another trustee observes, "I think we are faced with a transformation of our institutions through electronic information technology. It is not just incremental change; it is going to change us into an entirely different organization in many, many ways."

A president concludes that "the toughest thing we are faced with right now is technology. What effect is technology going to have administratively and instructionally within the college? How can technology be used to reach outside the college to deliver our programs? I think the board needs to require the institution to have a comprehensive technology plan." From another president comes the following: "I guess if I were to pick one issue, it would be the impact of change. By that I mean the impact of technology. I think that impact is going to change the face of the community college. It's going to change the way we deliver our services and to whom we deliver our services. I think the community college's role will be changed if the board does not understand the potential impact of those external changes."

Another president observes that the issue, aside from funding, is "trying to do things quite differently with education. People want to consume education differently, in shorter time frames, with more flexible arrangements via technology."

As someone wittily observed, change is our only constant. Trustees and presidents seem well aware of the need to interact with change, especially change brought about by the ever-evolving technologies.

Understanding and Advocating the Mission

An issue identified by trustees and presidents as extremely important is making sure the community college mission is protected, understood, and supported by its many constituents. Just as funding is a big umbrella under which many other issues reside, the community college mission similarly seems to have a propensity for attracting any number of issues under its broad structure. As has been said and implied many times in this book, the community college mission provides the philosophical base upon which all community college activities and functions rest.

The strategies to preserve the mission—as well as the solutions to resolve the issues associated with funding, technology, and change—are encompassed under the term *advocacy;* therefore, the solutions proposed for each issue will be addressed collectively. The fact that *advocacy* has been a favorite buzzword for presidents and trustees for the past two decades or so does not lessen its importance. Trustees and presidents must still be advocates for the community college, and what they are primarily advocating is the college's mission.

Mission. A trustee gets to the point quickly and states his case well: "I think the major issue facing the community college at any point in time, the next five years, the next 20 years, the last ten years, is maintaining its relevance to its constituency." In a similar vein, another trustee notes that "just being able to offer affordable education to the community and to the community college students" is critical. Another trustee surmises that "it's a tough question. But I would say the toughest issue we have as trustees is to make sure that we are meeting the needs of our local area."

A president states that "I just worry whether the community college, as adaptive and flexible as it has been in the past, will be able to turn the corner and not choke on its inability to adjust."

Promoting an understanding and support of the community college mission by the public remains an issue that trustees will have to deal with in the future. Much of the community college's success in the future will depend upon how well the mission is understood and supported by the public, and how well that support translates into actions such as the allocation of adequate resources to operate the college effectively.

Advocacy. Many of the solutions to the issues discussed above as well as any number of other issues facing the community college require that trustees serve as advocates for their own community college and for community colleges nationally. Those trustees interviewed understand the need to serve as advocates for the community college. Noting that the community college plays a critical role in preparing people for different jobs and different careers, one trustee believes that as a trustee it is her job to "see that the community college role is recognized both at the federal and state levels if we want people prepared for the workforce."

Similarly, another trustee believes that working with the legislative bodies is "where trustees should place major emphasis in the next four or five years." Yet another trustee believes that trustees must "communicate with our congressmen to stress the importance—the very real importance—of the community college to our community." One trustee realizes that "we [his college] have a problem and that problem is a lack of public awareness. People do not realize how many lives we affect just with our little community college."

Another trustee asserts that if the funding issue is to be resolved, trustees must "stay in close contact with legislators, and not just at the federal level; I am talking about state and even local levels. We must try to make them understand the problems with financing of education, and that is where our associations come into play. It has to be a team effort. I can talk to my local legislator, but if every other legislator is not going to pull in that direction, mine is not going to pull in that direction either." Another trustee believes that the only way to keep his community college viable is to "push our agenda with the legislature and with higher education boards as much as we can. Our president is in full agreement with that."

To conclude, a final comment offered by one trustee sums up the trustee's role with passion, intelligence, knowledge, and commitment:

> All trustees need right now to prepare themselves to go to Washington for our legislative seminar. We need advocacy. If we don't begin to understand the value of advocacy, we are going to lose. We as trustees have to understand why we want more computers. We [the community colleges] have to be competitive in the next few years. If we don't increase the maximum for Pell Grants in the next few years, we are going to lose. We need to get our students organized as one voice. They need to sit down and say what is going on. I think I have spilled my guts here. But we as trustees need to understand, to keep the college open, accessible, and focused on the job of re-educating the workforce. We need to continually know the purpose of a trustee. It is not a good ole boys' or girls' club. It is a job. It is important. And it is important that trustees understand what we are supposed to do and how we are supposed to do it.

REFERENCES

Brubacher, J.S. & Rudy, W. *Higher Education in Transition: A History of American Colleges and Universities, 1936–1968* (Rev. ed.). New York: Harper & Row, 1968.

Carver, J. & Mayhew, M. *A New Vision of Board Leadership: Governing the Community College.* Washington, DC: Association of Community College Trustees, 1994.

Drake, S.L. *Research Report: A Study of Community and Junior College Boards of Trustees.* Washington, DC: American Association of Community and Junior Colleges, Association of Community College Trustees, & Association of Governing Boards of Universities and Colleges, 1977.

Gillett-Karam, R., Roueche, S.D., & Roueche, J.E. *Under-representation and the Question of Diversity: Women and Minorities in the Community College.* Washington, DC: Community College Press, 1991.

Hughes, R.M. *A Manual for Trustees of Colleges and Universities* (3rd Ed.). Ames, IA: Iowa State College Press, 1951.

Kauffman, J. *At the Pleasure of the Board.* Washington, DC: American Council on Education, 1980.

Keeton, M. "The Constituencies and Their Claims." In G.L. Riley & J.V. Baldridge (Eds.), *Governing Academic Organizations: New Problems, New Perspectives.* Berkeley, CA: McCutchan Publishing Corporation, 1977 (pp. 194–210).

Kerr, C. *Troubled Times for American Higher Education: The 1990s and Beyond.* Albany, NY: State University of New York Press, 1994.

Kerr, C. & Gade, M.L. *The Guardians: Boards of Trustees and American Colleges and Universities.* Washington, DC: Association of Governing Boards of Universities and Colleges, 1989.

Nason, J.W. *The Nature of Trusteeship: The Role and Responsibilities of College and University Boards.* Washington, DC: Association of Governing Boards of Universities and Colleges, 1982.

Rauh, M.A. *The Trusteeship of Colleges and Universities.* New York: McGraw-Hill, 1969.

Rudolph, F. *The American College and University: A History* (Rev. Ed). Athens, GA: University of Georgia Press, 1990.

Vaughan, G.B. *The Community College Story: A Tale of American Innovation.* Washington, DC: American Association of Community Colleges, 1995.

Vaughan, G.B. *Leadership in Transition: The Community College Presidency.* New York: American Council on Education and MacMillan, 1989.

Vaughan, G.B. *The Community College Presidency.* New York: American Council on Education and MacMillan, 1986.

Vaughan, G.B., Mellander, G.A., & Blois, B. *The Community College Presidency: Current Status and Future Outlook.* Washington, DC: American Association of Community Colleges, 1994.

Vaughan, G.B., & Weisman, I.M. [community college president study]. Unpublished raw data, 1996.

Walker, D.E. *The Effective Administrator: A Practical Approach to Problem Solving, Decision Making, and Campus Leadership.* San Francisco: Jossey-Bass, 1986.

Whitmore, L.A. "Results of a National Survey of Local Community College Trustees: Trustee Characteristics." ACCT *Trustee Quarterly,* Fall 1987 (pp. 14–23).

Zoglin, M.L. *Power and Politics in the Community College.* Palm Springs, CA: ETC Publications, 1976.

DATE DUE
